The Research Paper Handbook

James D. Lester, Sr.
James D. Lester, Jr.

GoodYearBooks

An Imprint of ScottForesman
A Division of HarperCollins*Publishers*

Cover Illustration by Pat Dypold
Book Design by The Parker Group

GoodYearBooks are available for every basic curriculum subject
plus many enrichment areas. For more Good Year Books,
contact your local bookseller or educational dealer. For a
complete catalog, please write:

GoodYearBooks
Scott, Foresman and Company
1900 East Lake Avenue
Glenview, Illinois 60025

Acknowledgments
Page 62 "We Real Cool" by Gwendolyn Brooks,
from *Voices* by Geoffrey Summerfield, copyright 1969. Reprinted
by permission of the author.

Page 99 "The Skaters" by John Gould Fletcher, from *Adventures
in American Literature*, copyright 1985. Reprinted by permission
of Harcourt Brace Jovanovich.

ISBN 0-673-36016-4

9 RRD 99 98 97

Table of Contents

Chapter 11—APA Style   185

Appendix—Writing with Word Processing   208

Matters of Mechanics   217

Index   219

Chapter 1—Choosing a Topic

Begin your research project with a
well-focused subject. Your topic may be
anybody or anything—fashion, Nintendo
games, Andrew Jackson, electric motors.
Choose something that is interesting to
you—a topic you always have wanted to
learn more about, a question you want
answers to, an exploration into an area
that is entirely new.

1a Selecting and narrowing a subject

Select a topic with a built-in issue so that you can interpret the problem and cite the opinions of outside sources. When you do, you will bring a focus to your study and give yourself a reason for sharing outside sources with your readers. Each of the following topics addresses a problem or raises an issue:

`Children and Video Games: A Question of Addiction`

This topic raises two questions: Do children get addicted to video games? With what result?

`Andrew Jackson and the Trail of Tears`

This topic addresses a controversial issue: What was Andrew Jackson's role as president during the Trail of Tears?

Note: Avoid writing a summary of a person's life, retelling a piece of fiction, or copying an event of history from reference books.

Perhaps you will have no trouble in deciding on a topic. However, if you are not entirely sure of what to choose, try any of the following approaches: naming subtopics for a general topic, clustering, or asking questions about a topic.

Narrowing a general subject by naming subtopics

Start with a general idea and explore possible subtopics. Perhaps one item on the list can become your research topic. For example, start with biology lab and list subtopics, such as safety, waste disposal, and proper equipment. One of the subtopics might stimulate your thinking toward a topic with a built-in issue: "Biology labs need better equipment, especially to sterilize tools and protect students."

Exercise 1.1 Several general categories below are followed by subtopics. Under each general heading write two additional subtopics that interest you.

education

year-long school calendar
computers in school
teaching by television

_____

_____

history

John F. Kennedy
America's Civil War
Margaret Thatcher

_____

_____

sociology

day care centers
street gangs
teenagers as parents

_____

_____

medicine

treating teenage alcoholism
a nursing career
discovery of penicillin

_____

_____

literature

Robert Frost's poetry
Shakespeare's sonnets
Jackson's "The Lottery"

_____

_____

business

minimum wage
age discrimination
the stock market

_____

_____

popular culture

rock music lyrics
video games
horror movies

_____

_____

nature

insects
clean water
recycling programs

_____

_____

Narrowing a general subject by clustering

Some researchers begin with a general idea and cluster
ideas around it. Sometimes this technique is known as
creating "a web."

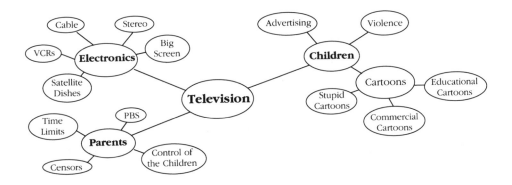

Exercise 1.2 Try your skill at clustering. Write your preliminary topic below inside the central circle and then begin creating your own web.

Narrowing a general subject by asking questions

A research question can serve two important functions. It can address a specific issue or problem that you may wish to investigate. It can also provoke an answer and thereby produce a possible thesis sentence. In either case, you will bring a focus to your entire paper (see **1b**, page 9). Here are a few examples of good research questions:

`Do immigrants today face the same kinds of`
`prejudice faced by immigrants 100 years ago?`

This topic poses a research issue and will require the writer to define prejudice and to cite evidence from source materials.

`How did Grant win the battle of Shiloh?`

This topic will require the writer to examine the historical facts and the opinions of military experts.

Do some parents spoil little league baseball for the girls and boys?

This topic has a built-in bias (the writer has seemingly reached a conclusion), yet it offers a chance for the writer to explore a sensitive issue, and perhaps interview both children and their parents.

Exercise 1.3 Listed below are research questions. Under each one check the appropriate box if **1)** the topic is well-focused and limited, **2)** the topic raises an issue or presents a problem worthy of examination, and **3)** the topic invites research into outside sources.

1. How does participation in the Boy Scouts and Girl Scouts contribute to the growth of young people?

Well-focused ☐   Raises an issue ☐

Invites research ☐

2. What is the *aurora borealis?*

Well-focused ☐   Raises an issue ☐

Invites research ☐

3. What really caused the corruption in Mark Twain's "The Man That Corrupted Hadleyburg"?

Well-focused ☐   Raises an issue ☐

Invites research ☐

4. Why do sports teams have mascots and nicknames?

Well-focused ☐   Raises an issue ☐

Invites research ☐

5. When did Oklahoma become a state?

Well-focused □ · Raises an issue □

Invites research □

6. Why must American drivers continue to depend on foreign oil?

Well-focused □ Raises an issue □

Invites research □

7. Do rules and regulations in our schools smother creativity in students?

Well-focused □ Raises an issue □

Invites research □

8. Why can't blacks and Hispanics and Asians use their native dialects in the classroom?

Well-focused □ Raises an issue □

Invites research □

9. Are dress codes really necessary in our schools?

Well-focused □ Raises an issue □

Invites research □

10. What is the standard for standardized tests? Who am I being judged against? Why?

Well-focused □ Raises an issue □

Invites research □

1b Developing a preliminary thesis sentence

A thesis sentence changes your topic or research question into a statement that you will support with your research. It presents a problem that you will examine with your evidence. It should go beyond the obvious. For example, almost everyone would agree with the following thesis statement, so no research is needed.

`Too much television is harmful to children.`

This sentence will not engage your readers because they know that excess in anything is harmful.

Instead, you should create a thesis sentence that is well-focused, raises an issue, and invites research.

`Violence in television cartoons can affect children.`

This sentence raises an issue. If you write a thesis sentence like this one, you would then need to research the subject, report your findings, and explain the effects of television violence on the children.

Exercise 1.4 Write the word *thesis* beside any sentence below that asserts something that will need investigation by the writer and require the citation of sources in the paper.

1. _____ Participation in the Scouts gives a girl or boy the chance to wear a nice uniform.

2. _____ A solar flare can affect the bright northern lights of the aurora borealis.

3. _____ Individual greed by the citizens caused the corruption of Mark Twain's imaginary town of Hadleyburg.

4. _____ Sports teams have mascots who often dress in weird costumes.

5. _____ Standardized tests cannot judge individual talent.

6. _____ Essay examinations are hard.

7. _____ Individuality is smothered by teachers who expect every student to conform to one standard of learning.

8. _____ Oklahoma became a state on November 16, 1907.

9. _____ Automakers resist any changes in the internal combustion engine, so our dependence on foreign oil will continue into the next century.

10. _____ Dress codes do not affect learning.

Use your thesis sentence to control and focus the entire paper and to tell the reader the point of your research.

You may change your working thesis at any time during the research because the evidence may lead you to new and different issues. However, your final thesis should meet several criteria. Use the following checklist to evaluate your final thesis:

Final Thesis Checklist

1. It expresses your position in a full, declarative sentence, is not a question, not a statement of purpose, and not merely a topic.

2. It reflects the fact that your paper is sharply focused on a single issue or topic.

3. It establishes an investigative, inventive edge to your research and thereby gives a reason for all your work.

4. It points forward to the conclusion.

If you have trouble discovering your thesis at first, ask yourself a few questions. The answer might very well be the thesis:

1. What is the point of my research?

`Recent research demonstrates that self-guilt often causes a teenager emotional problems.`

2. What do I want this paper to prove?

`Student clubs need school funding; students should not be required to sell products to raise funds.`

3. Can I tell the reader anything new or different?

Evidence indicates that advertisers have bought their way into the classroom with free educational materials.

4. Do I have a solution to the problem?

Public support for "safe" houses will provide a haven for children abused by their parents.

5. Do I have a new slant or new approach to the issue?

Personal economics is a force to be reckoned with, and poverty, not greed, forces many youngsters into a life of crime.

6. Should I take the minority view of this matter?

Give credit where it is due: Custer may have lost the battle at Little Bighorn, but Crazy Horse and his men, with inspiration from Sitting Bull, won the battle.

7. What exactly is my theory about this subject?

Trustworthy employees, not mechanical safeguards on computers and software, will prevent theft of software, sabotage of mainframes, and damaging viruses in the system.

Exercise 1.5 Listed on the next page are five thesis sentences. Can you write a question that each one answers? Example:

Thesis: Research papers stimulate the investigative mind.

Question: What purpose is served by research papers?

1. Recycling paper, plastic, and glass is justified at any cost.

Question:_____

_____

2. Public school athletic programs benefit schools in several ways.

Question:_____

_____

3. Jogging destroys a person's knees, ankles, and feet.

Question:_____

_____

4. Schools should convert to a year-long calendar.

Question:_____

_____

5. Love is not the most important ingredient in human relationships; respect is.

Question:_____

_____

1c Framing a research proposal

You probably will need to write a research proposal and have it approved by your instructor before beginning research in the library. The research proposal will give your work direction so that both your teacher and the librarian can serve your specific needs.

A research proposal is a short paragraph that identifies the essential ingredients of your work:

1. The purpose of the paper

2. The intended audience

3. Your role as a research writer

4. The thesis sentence

For example, one student writer developed this research proposal:

```
It saddens me to see people, even children,
throwing away their lives on cocaine addiction.
My role is to explain to my schoolmates the
effects of cocaine on various organs of the
body. I will defend this thesis: Cocaine will
not make you anything except dead, or almost
dead.
```

This writer identifies herself as a protester (role) against the use of cocaine (purpose). She will argue her idea (thesis) to her schoolmates (audience).

Establishing a purpose

Research papers do different things; they explain, analyze, and persuade—often in the same paper. A writer who argues against the use of drugs or smoking must also explain the products and analyze the different dangers.

Explanatory: Your purpose will be explanatory when you review and itemize factual information for your readers. One writer defined cocaine and explained how it came from the coca shrub of South America. Another writer explained how advertisers have gained entrance into classrooms by providing free educational materials.

Analytic: You will be analytical when you classify various parts of the subject in order to investigate each one in depth. One writer examined the effects of cocaine on the brain, the eyes, the lungs, the heart, and so on. Another writer classified and examined the methods used by advertisers to reach school children with their messages.

Persuasive: You will be persuasive when you address readers with a message of conviction that defends a position. One writer condemned the use of cocaine and warned of its dangers. Another writer argued that advertisers have enticed children into bad habits: poor eating, smoking, drinking, even violence.

Meeting the needs of your audience

You will want to design your paper for an academic audience, specifically your instructor and fellow students. You are addressing interested readers who expect a depth of understanding on your part and evidence of your background reading on the subject. Try to say something worthwhile by approaching the topic from your special point of view.

For example, the topic "latchkey children" can address children (to tell them to exercise caution), parents (to warn them to be vigilant in maintaining phone contact), and even school administrators (to ask them to consider extending the school day to serve the working parents).

Match the content of your paper with the needs of your readers. Are you boring them by retelling known facts from an encyclopedia or do you engage them with interesting comments on the evidence?

Recognizing your role as a researcher in the proposal

Your voice should show the nature of your work, to question, to examine, and to explore. Indicate the research you have already done by referring to authorities you have consulted. Offer quotations. Provide charts or graphs that you borrow from the sources. Your teachers will give you credit for using the sources in your paper. Just be certain that you give in-text citations to the sources to reflect your academic honesty. Your role is to investigate, explain, defend, and argue the issue at hand.

Expressing your thesis sentence in the proposal

Your preliminary thesis is an important part of the proposal because it sets in motion your examination of facts so that you can reach a conclusion. Your thesis will show the special nature of your paper. Note how four students arrived at different thesis sentences even though they had the same topic, "Santiago in Hemingway's *The Old Man and the Sea.*"

Note: This novel narrates the toils of an old Cuban fisherman named Santiago who has not caught a fish for many days. He desperately needs the money to be earned from a good catch. Finally, he catches a marlin and ties it to the side of his boat. However, sharks attack. By the time Santiago arrives home, he has only a skeleton of the fish.

Thesis: Poverty forced Santiago to venture too far and struggle beyond his strength in his attempt to land the giant fish.

This writer will examine Santiago's economic condition.

Thesis: The giant marlin is a symbol for all of life's obstacles and hurdles, and Santiago is a symbol for all suffering humans.

This writer will look at the religious and social symbolism of the novel.

Thesis: `Santiago represents a dying breed, the person who confronts alone the natural elements without modern technology.`

This writer will explore the history of fishing equipment and explain Santiago's failure in that light.

Thesis: `Hemingway's portrayal of Santiago demonstrates the author's deep respect for Cubans and Cuba, where he lived for many years.`

This writer will examine the Cuban culture and its influence on Hemingway.

Exercise 1.6 Use the checklist below to identify your reasons for writing your research paper. You may, and probably should, mark more than one.

- ☐ I want to explain the subject.
- ☐ I want to classify the parts and offer ideas about them.
- ☐ I want to argue a position.

Now complete the following sentences with specific thoughts about your research topic.

I want to explain to readers my general findings about_____

_____.

I want to offer readers my classification and analysis of these items:_____

_____.

I want to convince my readers about my position on_____

_____.

Before writing your own proposal, study the following two research proposals. Underline and label the purpose, writer's role, audience, and thesis in each.

I want to investigate the life of Martin Luther King, Jr. in order to explain his life to other young persons and to list the reasons for his mission in life. I want to endorse his overwhelming commitment to the civil rights movement.

I want art students to understand that Leonardo da Vinci was one of the greatest painters of the Renaissance. My job is to defend da Vinci and argue that his genius contributed to art, science, literature, religion, and engineering.

In the space below write your own research proposal and submit it to your instructor.

_____

_____

_____

_____

_____

Chapter 2—Using the Card Catalog and Reference Indexes

This chapter explains how to select and record information about the books and articles that you will need to read. After your research proposal is approved, you can begin a systematic, three-phase search in the library. Remember, a well–written research paper will be based on more than one or two encyclopedia articles.

Phase 1. Preliminary search of: the subject cards of the card catalog, reference books, bibliographies, indexes, and any available computer sources.

Phase 2. Narrowing by: browsing, skimming books and articles, selecting citations from materials that you will read.

Phase 3. Reading and note-taking from: books, essays, articles, computer printouts, abstracts, and other sources.

Writing from sources is a serious task that will take time. Depend on your librarian for help. Some leads will have dead ends; some research will be duplicated. Don't be discouraged. Expect to go back and forth from reading to searching the indexes and back again to reading. Your task is not only to find sources but to make appropriate selections from the sources.

2a Learning about your library and its resources

What is the best source of information in the library? The card catalog? The *Readers' Guide to Periodical Literature?* An encyclopedia? While they can all be useful, the best single source is your librarian who will help you become familiar with your library's full range of sources and services.

Circulation desk. Go here for directions and to check out your books. Whenever you cannot find a book on your own, check at the circulation desk to determine whether it is checked out, on reserve, or lost. If the book is checked out, you may place a hold order and the librarian will contact you when the book is returned. The circulation desk also handles most general business: renewals, collection of fines, and access to special collections and various machines (video cassette recorders, photocopying, computers).

Computer facilities. Modern technology has eased the search for sources: card catalogs now appear on computers, data base information is available by telephone transmission, and compact disks within computers can search several volumes of *Readers' Guide to Periodical Literature* for you and provide a printout. Use this new technology whenever possible. You will discover how quick and efficient it can be. (See **2c**, page 35, for complete details).

Reference section. After your research proposal is approved, you will also want to use your library's reference section where you will find the bibliographies and indexes for your search of information sources. Here you can develop a set of bibliography cards that will direct you to books and articles.

Periodical sections. This is where you will find newspapers and magazines. You will be able to read many of the articles you need on microfilm rather than in bound volumes.

Vertical files. These files contain articles clipped from magazines and newspapers. They are kept in alphabetical order by topic, not by title. You may find several articles on your topic at once.

Reserve desk. Instructors often place books and articles on reserve for short loan periods—from a few hours to a day or two—so that more students will have access to them. This system prevents one student from keeping an important, even crucial, book for a week or more while others need it. Your library may also place on reserve other valuable items that might be subject to theft, such as recordings, video tapes and statistical information.

Card catalog. All of the library's resources are listed in the card catalog by author, title, and subject—all interfiled in one alphabetical system (see **2b**, page 25). Some libraries have updated the card catalog system to either microfilm systems or computer terminals (see **2b**, page 25 and **2c**, page 35).

Stacks. The shelves of the library hold books where you can locate specific works by call numbers and perhaps browse for other books that interest you. However, some libraries will not permit you into this area. Instead, you have to provide the call number(s) for an attendant who will go into the stacks for you.

Interlibrary loans. Libraries borrow from one another. The interlibrary loan service thereby supplements a library's resources by making materials available from other libraries. Understand, however, that receiving a book or article by interlibrary loan may take several days.

Photocopiers. Photocopying services provide a real convenience, enabling you to take home articles from journals and from reserve books that you cannot withdraw from the library. However, copyright laws protect authors and place certain restrictions on the library. You may use the copying machines and duplicating services for your own individual purposes, but be sure that you give proper credit to the sources (see Chapter 5).

Exercise 2.1 On a blank sheet of paper draw a rough sketch of your library to show the location of the circulation desk, computer facilities (if available), reference section, reserve desk (if it differs from the circulation desk), card catalog, stacks, photocopy machines, vertical files, and periodical section.

2b Using the card catalog

The card catalog lists all books in your library by title, by last name of the author, and by subject. You should start your search by examining the subject heading on the cards, or, when available, by typing in your subject at the on-line public access catalog (PAC). In either case, the catalog will index all the books in your library that include coverage of your topic, such as TOYS, CHILDREN, or PARENTS. The cards or entries will include the book's call number, author, title, place and date of publication, publisher, and any notes on its contents. A card may also include chapter titles; names of editors, compilers, or translations; volume number and/or series name.

Fig. 1: Sample subject card

```
305.4      WOMEN
0973       Rappaport, Doreen.
R36a
           American women: their lives in their words.
           New York: Thomas Y. Crowell [1990]


           Includes bibliographical references.
           Summary: Excerpts from women's diaries, letters,
           speeches, and autobiographical writings provide a
           first-person look at the history of American women


           ISBN 0-690-04819-X
           1. Women--United States--History--Sources
           HQ1410.R36 1990 305.4'0973
```

Fig. 2: Sample handwritten bibliography card to a book. Note the call number, author, title, place and date of publication, publisher, and a note on the book's contents.

305.4 / 0973 / R36a

Rappaport, Doreen
    American Women: Their Lives
in Their Words. New York:
Crowell, 1990.

        has a bibliography

You will need these cards to help you locate the books you want to investigate, and later, to compile your "Words Cited" (see page 141).

If you are working with a PAC, order a printout of the books on your topic. It is likely to look something like this:

Fig. 3: Sample PAC printout to library books.

```
Keyword Search Request: Women

Bibliographic record--No. 6 of 12 entries found

Saidman, Anne.
        Oprah Winfrey: Media success story.--1st ed. New York: Lerner  Pub., 1990.
        Subject Headings: Winfrey, Oprah / Television personalities /
                Motion picture actors and actresses / Afro-American-Biography
        LOCATION: History stacks
        CALL NUMBER: PN1992.4 S25
```

Learning to read a catalog card

A catalog card contains essential information that you must copy to your own bibliography card. You can also write it at the top of a notebook page (you can then use the rest of the page for notes from the source). To find a book in the stacks, you need only the call number, author, and title. But later on, if you paraphrase or quote the book in your paper, you will need additional information for the bibliography entry on your "Works Cited" page, such as place, publisher, and date of publication. In some cases, you will need other information, such as the edition (other than the first), editor(s), translator, and so forth (see pages 142–152 for additional examples). Shown below are a catalog card and a matching bibliography card in MLA (Modern Language Association) style.

Fig. 4: Catalog Card
1) Call number
2) author
3) title **4)** coauthor
5) place of publication
6) publisher
7) date of publication
8) technical description
9) note on contents
of the book **10)** separate
card filed under subject
heading as well as under
names of coauthor and
the title **11)** Library of
Congress call number
12) Dewey Decimal
number **13)** Order
number **14)** Publisher
of this card

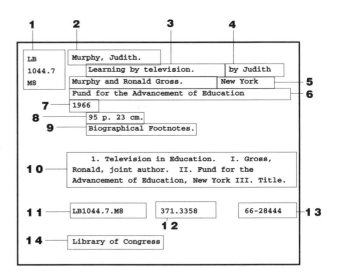

Fig. 5: Sample
bibliography card
of basic information:
Copy only the call
number, author(s),
title, place of
publication,
publisher,
year of publication.

*LB / 1044.7 / 118
Murphy, Judith, and
Ronald Gross.
Learning By
Television. New
York: Fund for
Adv. of Ed., 1966.*

Use the following order for writing information onto
your bibliography card (1, 3, and 8 are required)

1. Author(s)

2. Chapter or part of a book

3. Title of the book

4. Editor, translator, or compiler

5. Edition other than first

6. Number of volumes

7. Name of the series

8. Publisher, place and date of publication

9. Volume number of this book

10. Page numbers to a chapter or part of the book

Note: See Chapter 9, "Works Cited," for ways to write the various bibliography forms for a book, magazine, interview, and so forth.

If you use the PAC printout for your search, there is no need to write a bibliography card. Later, if you use a source, you can write a proper entry for the "Works Cited" page (see page 149).

Fig. 6: PAC entry

```
Keyword Search Request: Television and Children
Bibliographic record -- No. 3 of 3 entries


Palmer, Edward L.
        Television and America's children: a crisis of neglect / Edward L. Palmer.
        New York: Oxford University Press, 1988.
        xxv, 194 p. ; 22 cm Includes index.
SUBJECT HEADINGS
        Television programs for Children
        Public television
        Children's television workshop
LOCATION: Main Library
CALL NUMBER: PN1992.9 C46 P36
```

Exercise 2.2 Write a bibliography entry for the following catalog entry. *Note: List only the call number, the names of the joint authors, the place and date of publication, and the publisher.* See the examples on page 28 for the correct form.

```
        MONEY

332     Gurley. John G.
G8m     Money in a theory of finance, by John G. Gurley and
        Edward S.Shaw.  New York: Macmillan, 1988


        xiv, 317 p. illus. 24 cm.
        Bibliographical footnotes.
        1. Finance. 2. Money. 3. Shaw, Edward Stone, joint author
        4. Title


        HG173.G8 332 60-798
```

Exercise 2.3 Write a bibliography entry based on
information found in the PAC entry on the following
page. *Note: List call number, author, title, place of
publication, publisher, and year.*

Fig. 7: PAC entry

```
Touchstone, Pamela
        TV violence: the threat to the children.
        New York: Grogan Publishing House, 1991.
Bibliography : p. 3301-314 / Includes index.
SUBJECT HEADINGS:
        Television and children
        Interactive television

LOCATION: EDUCATION STACKS
CALL NUMBER: 372/T17t
```

Distinguishing the Dewey decimal and the LC systems

Your library will classify its books by one of two systems, the Dewey decimal system or the Library of Congress (LC) system. The Dewey system would list Murphy's *Learning by Television* (see Fig. 4) with the number "371.3358," but the LC system uses "LB 1044.7.M8." Understanding the system of your library will prove helpful to you as your proceed in writing your research paper.

The Dewey decimal system. Figure 8 shows the complete 100 divisions of the Dewey system.

Fig. 8: From the *Dewey Decimal Classification and Relative Index*

Second Summary*
The Hundred Divisions

000	**Generalities**	**500**	**Natural sciences & mathematics**
010	Bibliography	510	Mathematics
020	Library & information sciences	520	Astronomy & allied sciences
030	General encyclopedic works	530	Physics
040		540	Chemistry & allied sciences
050	General serials & their indexes	550	Earth sciences
060	General organizations & museology	560	Paleontology Paleozoology
070	News media, journalism, publishing	570	Life sciences
080	General collections	580	Botanical sciences
090	Manuscripts & rare books	590	Zoological sciences
100	**Philosophy & psychology**	**600**	**Technology (Applied sciences)**
110	Metaphysics	610	Medical sciences Medicine
120	Epistemology, causation, humankind	620	Engineering & allied operations
130	Paranormal phenomena	630	Agriculture
140	Specific philosophical schools	640	Home economics & family living
150	Psychology	650	Management & auxiliary services
160	Logic	660	Chemical engineering
170	Ethics (Moral philosophy)	670	Manufacturing
180	Ancient, medieval, Oriental philosophy	680	Manufacture for specific uses
190	Modern Western philosophy	690	Buildings
200	**Religion**	**700**	**The arts**
210	Natural theology	710	Civic & landscape art
220	Bible	720	Architecture
230	Christian theology	730	Plastic arts Sculpture
240	Christian moral & devotional theology	740	Drawing & decorative arts
250	Christian orders & local church	750	Painting & paintings
260	Christian social theology	760	Graphic arts Printmaking & prints
270	Christian church history	770	Photography & photographs
280	Christian denominations & sects	780	Music
290	Other & comparative religions	790	Recreational & performing arts
300	**Social sciences**	**800**	**Literature & rhetoric**
310	General statistics	810	American literature in English
320	Political science	820	English & Old English literatures
330	Economics	830	Literatures of Germanic languages
340	Law	840	Literatures of Romance languages
350	Public administration	850	Italian, Romanian, Rhaeto-Romanic
360	Social services; association	860	Spanish & Portuguese literatures
370	Education	870	Italic literatures Latin
380	Commerce, communications, transport	880	Hellenic literatures Classical Greek
390	Customs, etiquette, folklore	890	Literatures of other languages
400	**Language**	**900**	**Geography & history**
410	Linguistics	910	Geography & travel
420	English & Old English	920	Biography, genealogy, insignia
430	Germanic languages German	930	History of ancient world
440	Romance languages French	940	General history of Europe
450	Italian, Romanian, Rhaeto-Romanic	950	General history of Asia Far East
460	Spanish & Portuguese languages	960	General history of Africa
470	Italic languages Latin	970	General history of North America
480	Hellenic languages Classical Greek	980	General history of South America
490	Other languages	990	General history of other areas

*Consult schedules for complete and exact headings

*Note: The 300 category is labeled **Social Sciences,** and it lists this subdivision: **370 Education.** The Murphy book (Fig. 4) belongs to this category and is designated **371.3358.***

Immediately below the Dewey classification numbers you will see a second line of letters and numerals based on the Cutter Three-Figure Author Table. For example, **M954L** is the author number for Murphy's *Learning by Television.* The letter **M** is the initial of the author's last name. Next, the Cutter table subclassifies with the number **954,** and the lowercase **L** designates the first important letter in the title to distinguish this entry from similar books by Murphy. Thus, the complete call number for Murphy's book is **371.3358/M954L.**

You will need the entire set of numbers to locate the book. Most high school libraries use the Dewey Decimal call numbers. Most college libraries use the Library of Congress call numbers. A catalog card often features both sets of numbers: LB1044.7/M8/371.3358 means LC number, Cutter author number, and Dewey Decimal number.

Library of Congress (LC) classification system. The LC system also uses a combination of letters and numerals. The major divisions are shown on the following page.

Fig. 9: From the Library of Congress System

LIBRARY OF CONGRESS CLASSIFICATION SCHEDULES

For sale by the Cataloging Distribution Service, Library of Congress, Building 159, Navy Yard Annex, Washington, D.C. 20541, to which inquiries on current availability and price should be addressed.

A	General Works
B-BJ	Philosophy, Psychology
BL-BX	Religion
C	Auxiliary Sciences of History
D	History: General and Old World (Eastern Hemisphere)
E-F	History: America (Western Hemisphere)
G	Geography, Maps, Anthropology, Recreation
H	Social Sciences
J	Political Science
K	Law (General)
KD	Law of the United Kingdom and Ireland
KE	Law of Canada
KF	Law of the United States
L	Education
M	Music
N	Fine Arts
P-PA	General Philology and Linguistics. Classical Languages and Literatures
PA Supplement	Byzantine and Modern Greek Literature. Medieval and Modern Latin Literature
PB-PH	Modern European Languages
PG	Russian Literature
PJ-PM	Languages and Literatures of Asia, Africa, Oceania. American Indian Languages. Artifical Languages
P-PM Supplement	Index to Languages and Dialects
PN, PR, PS, PZ	General Literature. English and American Literature. Fiction in English. Juvenile Belles Lettres
PQ Part 1	French Literature
PQ Part 2	Italian, Spanish, and Portuguese Literatures
PT Part 1	German Literature
PT Part 2	Dutch and Scandinavian Literatures
Q	Science
R	Medicine
S	Agriculture
T	Technology
U	Military Science
V	Naval Science
Z	Bibliography. Library Science

*Note: **L** designates "Education." Accordingly, Murphy's book is assigned **L** with the subentries **B1044.7.** Then, like the Cutter system, LC uses the first letter of the author's name and a subnumber, **M8.***

Another example of these systems follows:

Howard E. Hesketh. *Understanding and Controlling Air Pollution.* 2nd ed. Ann Arbor: Ann Arbor Science, 1974.

Library of Congress	**Dewey decimal**
TD [Environmental Technology]	628.53 [Engineering & allied operations]
833 [Air Pollution]	H461u [Author Number]
H48	

By using either set of numbers, depending upon your library, you would find this book.

Exercise 2.4 Identify the following call numbers by labeling them *LC* or *Dewey*:

1. _____	2. _____	3. _____	4. _____
220.654	DC	930.376	BL
G398b	435	L211g	142
	L543		G309

2c Learning to use a computer search

Many software programs have academic applications. Microcomputers can now be used to search library files. For instance, rather than search the printed volumes of *Readers' Guide to Periodical Literature*, students at many public school libraries and most college libraries can now scan computer screens to quickly survey several different subjects and subtopics.

If the computer list looks promising, they can immediately get a printout and go in search of books and articles. The day approaches when bulky printed indexes will be replaced by compact disks and computer printouts. If it is up-to-date, your library will have one or more of these features:

On-line public access catalog (PAC). (See also, **9c**, pages 149-150, for a discussion and additional examples) The PAC gives you the card catalog on a computer disk. You can quickly get a printout of books on a given subject or a list of all the books by one or more authors. You will even find out if the books are available. Here is an example of a printout on the subject of Ernest Hemingway's story *"The Old Man and the Sea"*:

Jobes, Katharine T., ed.
Twentieth century interpretations of The old man and the sea: a collection of critical essays. Englewood Cliffs, N. J. Prentice-Hall (1968)
SUBJECT HEADING: Hemingway, Ernest, 1899-1961.
LOCATION: MAIN LIBRARY
CALL NUMBER PS3515.E37
CHECKED OUT TO A USER. Due 05/01/91

Hemingway, Ernest.
The old man and sea. New York: Scribner's, 1952.
LOCATION: MAIN LIBRARY
CALL NUMBER: PZ3.H3736
Not checked out. If not on shelf, ask at circulation desk.

Compact disks stored in computers (CD-ROM).
Some libraries have CD-ROM facilities, which means they have data base files such as *Readers' Guide to Periodical Literature* located on a compact disk stored as *read only memory* (ROM) in the computer. ROM means the computer can read the files for you, but nobody can write into the files to change them. Use the CD-ROM files to find articles in such periodicals as *American Health, Business Week, Current History, Discover, Ebony, Health, Ms., Newsweek, Omni, Science News, and many other*s. (See also **2e**, pages 44-47, for additional discussion with examples.)

The CD-ROM terminal will provide you with a printout of sources. One student, for example, was concerned about the condition of elephants confined within zoos. He requested articles that matched *elephant* and *zoo* and found that seven matches existed:

```
AAAAAAAAAAAAAAAAAAAAAAAAAAAAAAAAAAAAAAAAAAAA
Search set          Wilsearch Command    No. of postings
AAAAAAAAAAAAAAAAAAAAAAAAAAAAAAAAAAAAAAAAAAAA
1                   FIND ELEPHANT        34
2                   FIND ZOO             28
-                   FIND 1 AND 2

                              7 MATCHES

AAAAAAAAAAAAAAAAAAAAAAAAAAAAAAAAAAAAAAAAAAAA
```

The student could then browse through the seven items and order a printout of any that appeared appropriate, such as this one:

```
4. Tisdale, Sallie
        The only harmless great thing (Asian elephant breeding
        research at Washington Park Zoo)
        The New Yorker v64 p38-40+ January 23 '89
```

On-line data bases with telephone modems. A data base search means that you or a librarian must connect the library's computer by phone modem to a national data base vendor, such as DIALOG. The vendor will then transmit data from specific data bases. Here are a few major data bases to consider:

ERIC (Educational Resources Information Center) will help with papers in such fields as education, ethnic studies, health, physical education, psychology, speech, women's studies.

MLA BIBLIOGRAPHY (Modern Language Association) will help with papers in language and literature.

SCISEARCH will help with papers in biology, chemistry, environmental studies, geology, physics.

SOCIAL SCISEARCH will help with papers in economics, ethnic studies, geography, history, philosophy, political science, speech, women's studies. Even the Cable News Network (CNN) is available through an on-line phone modem. *Note: you may be required to pay a fee for data base services.*

An on-line data base search involves several steps. For example, one writer went in search of sources on the topic "Acne." He focused on creams, drugs, and other medication. He filed a "Search Request" to answer such questions as these:

1. What title would best describe the paper's content?

2. What are the specific topics, synonyms, closely related phrases, and alternate spellings of the subject, using scientific, technical, and common names?

3. What related topics should be excluded in order to narrow the search?

4. Should foreign language entries be included? Which languages?

5. Should citations be limited to a specific publication year(s)?

The purpose of this questionnaire should be fairly obvious: the computer operator needs terminology to feed into the data base file. Usually three key terms are needed to control a search of the sources:

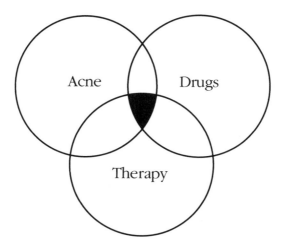

The computer will search through records to select only those that match the darkened area—which will be books and articles that feature the three key terms.

The computer will then produce a printout of those sources that will look something like Figure 10, below:

Fig. 10: A Data Base Search

09073338 Dialog File 149: Health Periodicals Database

TITLE: Acne: taming that age-old adolescent affliction.
AUTHOR: Sharon Snider
JOURNAL: FDA Consumer VOL: V24 Issue: n8 PAGINATION: 16(4)
PUBLICATION DATE: Oct. 1990
AVAILABILITY: FULL TEXT Online LINE COUNT 00146
SPECIAL FEATURES: illustration; photograph
SOURCE FILE: MI File 47
PRODUCT NAMES(S): Retin-A; Accutane

In this case, you can order a printout of the full text. (There will be a fee charged, however.) For other sources only a printout of the abstract is available on-line, noted by this message: ABSTRACT AVAILABLE.

When an abstract is available, order a printout. You can cite from the abstract just as you would from the complete article (see Chapter 5).

ABSTRACT: Isotretinoin (Accutane) is a medication used for severe, cystic acne that has not been alleviated by other treatments and will most likely cause scarring if left untreated. The drug is not appropriate for patients with less severe acne, as there are other medications available that are preferable. The most troubling side effect of isotretinoin is the risk of birth defects and spontaneous abortions if taken by pregnant women. The teratongenic (causing fetal abnormalities) effect of the drug was recognized before marketing, and the manufacturer took measures to inform physicians and patients that the drug should not be taken during pregnancy. While the drug packaging has always contained a warning, additional abortions have dropped substantially since the first 18 months of the drug's availability; there were 17 birth defects and 20 miscarriages reported at this time. Birth defects associated with isotretinoin numbered four in 1989, three in 1988, 10 in 1987 and 12 in 1986. Experts disagree about the potential number of unreported birth defects linked with this antiacne drug. A study is underway to follow over 31,000 women who are using isotretinoin; to date, almost all of these patients have been aware of the importance of preventing pregnancy while taking isotretinoin. Additional steps proposed to ensure antiacne drug used only in appropriate patient population. By Charles Marwick v 263 *JAMA, The Journal of the American Medication Association* June 20 90 P3125(2)

Data base files change almost monthly, so depend on your librarian to suggest an appropriate data base for your project.

Using the microfilm

Libraries have a choice when ordering periodicals: they can buy expensive printed volumes or purchase inexpensive microfilm versions of the same material. Most libraries have a mixture of the two. In particular, most libraries now store national newspapers, weekly magazines, abstracts, and some journals on microfilm. Use a film reader, usually located near the microfilm files, to browse the articles. Should you need a printed copy of a microfilmed article, the library will copy it for you on a film printer.

Rather than develop a set of bibliography cards, write each source at the top of a sheet of notebook paper. Then use each sheet for notes from that one source.

2d Learning how to use a printed index to periodical literature

An index provides you with exact page numbers to an article in a periodical, newspaper, or book. An index is usually alphabetized by subject, author, and title. Most school libraries have *Readers' Guide to Periodical Literature* (or the abridged version). Here is an example accompanied by a student's note card:

Acne
Acne: taming that age-old adolescent affliction. S. Snider. il. *FDA Consumer 24; 16-19 O '90*

> *Snider, A.*
> *"Acne: Taming That*
> *Age-Old Adolescent*
> *Affliction." FDA*
> *Consumer Oct. 1990:*
> *16-19.*

A CD-ROM terminal (see **2c**) will provide you with a printout of this same information if your library has the facilities.

Fig. 12: Printout from *InfoTrac*

1. Acne: taming that age-old adolescent affliction. by Sharon Snider il v24 FDA Consumer Oct '90 p16(4)

Exercise 2.5 Write a bibliography card based on information found in the following entry from *Readers' Guide to Periodical Literature:*

Unbeatable buck? P. Duggan. il *Forbes* 145:76 Ja 22 '90.

Exercise 2.6 Write a bibliography card for the following source from a CD-ROM terminal:

Fears about acne drug: are warnings enough to prevent birth defects? (Accutane) by Matt Clark il v111 Newsweek May 2 '88 p66

2e Developing bibliography cards from other sources

Books (found through the card catalog) and periodical articles (found through an index such as *Readers' Guide to Periodical Literature*) are only part of any library's holdings. Look at newspapers, encyclopedias, biographical dictionaries, and handbooks.

In addition, do some of your research outside the library. Watch a television program, attend a lecture, interview somebody, request information by letter, or conduct a survey by means of a carefully crafted questionnaire. In every case, you must also prepare a bibliography entry that indicates the type of source used.

Newspaper. If you take notes from a newspaper article, write a bibliography entry. Here is a sample bibliography card for an article in *USA Today*. It requires the author, title of the article, title of the newspaper, date, and page numbers to the specific section.

Peterson, Karen S. "Positive Thinking Gives Kids a Lift." *USA Today* 19 Sept. 1990: 9A.

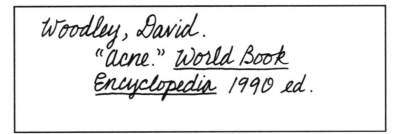

Encyclopedia. If you read and take notes from an encyclopedia article or biographical dictionary, make a bibliography entry like this:

If no author is listed, start with the title of the article. Remember, however, that authors are often mentioned at the end of encyclopedia articles by full names or by initials. The initials will be explained elsewhere, probably in another volume of the encyclopedia set, so go search out the full name.

Television, videotape, audiotape. If you borrow ideas from any type of audiovisual material, note carefully the source and cite specific catalog numbers.

Long Day's Journey into Night
 Republic Pictures Video
 VHS
 V2433.
 1985.

Sophocles. *Oedipus Rex*.
 Corinth Video. Trans.
 W.B. Yeats. 1957;
 1985. PA 4414.

"Hooded Seals."
 Profiles
 of Nature. Discovery
 Channel. 18 Sept. 1990.

Interview, letter, miscellaneous unpublished sources. If you interview somebody and plan to use their words or ideas, write a bibliography card that lists the person, the type of information, the place, and the date. If appropriate, add other pertinent information.

Robertson, Jason.
 Interview. Indianapolis,
 12 Sept.
 1991.

Beach, M.B. Private
 papers and letters.
 Springfield, 15 Jan.
 1990.

Thompson, Roland.
 "The
 Tropical Rain Forests."
 Lecture. Bakersfield,
 3 March 1991.

Exercise 2.7 Write a bibliography entry for the following information to an article in *The New York Times:*

Molly O'Neill's article entitled "What to Put in the Pot: Cooks Face Challenge over Animal Rights." From *The New York Times,* Wednesday, August 8, 1990, pages C1 and C6.

Exercise 2.8 Write a bibliography entry for the following information:

An article entitled "Eastwood, Clint" that appears in alphabetical order in *Current Biography Yearbook,* published in 1989.

Exercise 2.9 Write a bibliography entry for the following information:

"News Special," *CBS News,* CBS-TV, April 5, 1991.

Exercise 2.10 Write a bibliography entry for the following information:

A personal letter addressed to you from Mobile, Alabama, from Marcia C. Cartwright, dated October 10, 1990.

Chapter 3—Taking Notes

A well-written research paper is built on carefully written notes. This chapter explains how to record information onto note cards. Using primary and secondary sources, you can take notes using direct quotations, paraphrase, summaries, and personal notes.

As you explore information sources, you will need to write different kinds of notes:

- Use **direct quotations** to copy the exact words from the sources
- Use **summaries** to condense the ideas of others

- Use **paraphrase** to rewrite in your own words the ideas of another person

- Develop plenty of **personal notes** that record your own thoughts

Each of your notes should include the author and the pages you used in writing your notes. You do not need to include other data which is already recorded on your bibliography card.

3a Writing direct quotation note cards

The easiest type of note is one that copies the words of another person. However, you must be careful to follow a few rules:

1) You cannot copy the words of a source into your paper in such a way that readers will think *you* wrote the material.

2) You must use exactly the same words you found in the source.

3) You must provide an in-text citation to the author and page number, like this: (Lester 34–35). (See Chapter 5 for a thorough discussion of in-text citations.)

4) You may and often should give the author's name at the beginning of the quotation and use the in-text citation for page number only, like this:

```
Fred V. Hein says, "The human body, with its
unique blend of cells, tissues, organs, and
systems, is the most complex and intricate
living-machine yet observed on earth" (16).
```

5) You must begin every quotation with a quotation mark and end it with a quotation mark, as shown above.

6) The in-text citation goes *outside* the quotation mark but *inside* the final period.

7) The quoted material should be important and well-phrased, not something trivial or something that is common knowledge. NOT "John F. Kennedy was a Democrat from Massachusetts" (Rupert 233), but "John F. Kennedy's Peace Corps left a legacy of lasting compassion for the downtrodden" (Rupert 233).

Show the evidence of your research by using the names and page numbers of sources; let readers see the results of your notetaking from books and articles.

Exercise 3.1 Remember, direct quotations must include the exact words found in the source with quotation marks on both sides of the quotation, and the page(s) where the quotation was found. Direct quotations should not include trivial information. Five quotation notes are shown below that are based on this original material from an encyclopedia:

Dickens, Charles (1812–1870), was a great English novelist and one of the most popular writers of all time. His best-known books include *A Christmas Carol, David Copperfield, Great Expectations, Oliver Twist, The Pickwick Papers,* and *A Tale of Two Cities.* Dickens created some of the most famous characters in English literature. He also created scenes and descriptions of places that have delighted readers for more than a hundred years. Dickens was a keen observer of life, and had a great understanding of people. He showed sympathy for the poor and helpless, and mocked and criticized the selfish, the greedy, and the cruel.—Richard D. Altick, *The World Book Encyclopedia.*

Evaluate the merits of these notes according to the seven criteria above. Any *no* answer means that the given note is unacceptable.

A. **According to Richard Altick, "Dickens was a keen observer of life, and he had a great understanding of people. He showed sympathy for the poor and helpless, and mocked and criticized the selfish, the greedy, and the cruel" (D–154).**

1._____	2._____	3._____	4._____	5._____
Exact words	Cites author and page	Uses quotation marks	Page citation is outside the quotation mark but inside the period	Material is well-phrased and worthy of quotation

B. Charles Dickens was a "great English novelist and one of the most popular writers of all time."

1._____	2._____	3._____	4._____	5._____
Exact words	Cites author and page	Uses quotation marks	Page citation is outside the quotation mark but inside the period	Material is well-phrased and worthy of quotation

C. According to Richard Altick, Charles Dickens "was a great English novelist" (D-154).

1._____	2._____	3._____	4._____	5._____
Exact words	Cites author and page	Uses quotation marks	Page citation is outside the quotation mark but inside the period	Material is well-phrased and worthy of quotation

D. Charles Dickens was a keen observer of life, and had a great understanding of people. He showed sympathy for the poor and helpless, and mocked and criticized the selfish, the greedy, and the cruel (Altick D-154).

1._____	2._____	3._____	4._____	5._____
Exact words	Cites author and page	Uses quotation marks	Page citation is outside the quotation mark but inside the period	Material is well-phrased and worthy of quotation

E. In books such as *A Christmas Carol, Oliver Twist,* and *A Tale of Two Cities,* Charles Dickens "was a keen observer of life, and had a great understanding of people" (Altick D-154).

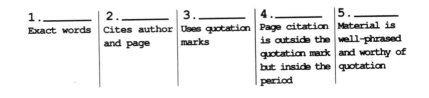

1._____	2._____	3._____	4._____	5._____
Exact words	Cites author and page	Uses quotation marks	Page citation is outside the quotation mark but inside the period	Material is well-phrased and worthy of quotation

3b Writing summary note cards

A summary captures in just a few words the key idea of a paragraph, outlines an entire article, or provides a summary of a complete book. It has specific uses.

Plot summary. As a service to your reader, you might include a very brief summary of a novel or story:

Great Expectations by Dickens describes young Pip, who inherits money and can live the life of a gentleman. But he discovers that his "great expectations" have come from a criminal. With that knowledge his attitude changes from one of vanity to one of compassion.

Review. A quick review of an article serves two purposes. In one case, you merely scan a piece of writing to jot down a few essentials in case you want to come back and read it carefully:

Altick's article describes the life of Dickens,
his books, and his place in literature.

In another type of review, you may need to write a
quick note to explain something special about the
work.

The biography <u>Andrew Jackson</u>, by James C.
Curtis, describes a president who was always
full of mistrust. Curtis subtitles the book as
<u>The Search for Vindication</u>, which means that
Jackson lived his life trying to justify his
public acts and to defend his personal life.

*Note: A summary needs no citation to a page number
because a summary reviews the entire work, not a
specific passage.*

Abstract. An abstract is a brief summary of one's own
paper. It is often required for a paper written in APA
style (see Chapter 11). It appears at the beginning of
the paper, and it helps readers decide to read or to skip
an article. You will see entire books devoted to
abstracts, such as *Psychological Abstracts* or *Abstracts of
English Studies.* Here is an example:

This study examines the problems of child abuse, especially the
fact that families receive attention after abuse occurs, not before.
With statistics on the rise, efforts devoted to prevention rather
than coping should focus on parents in order to discover those
adults who are most likely to commit abuse because of heredity,
their own childhood, the economy, and other causes of
depression. Viewing the parent as a victim, not just a criminal,
will enable social agencies to institute preventive programs that
may control abuse and hold together family units.

Exercise 3.2 Shown below are four summary notes. Select the label that best describes the nature of the summary—*plot summary, review,* or *abstract.*

1) Erikson devotes several chapters of his book *Toys and Reasons* to the play rituals in one's life cycle, from the toy age of preschoolers all the way up to adults and their toys.

___ plot summary   ___ review   ___ abstract

2) This article will explain that children do watch television, so teachers should respond to the electronic revolution. The authors argue that television is another tool for education, but it will be an effective tool only if teachers develop a television consciousness and use the media as a supplement to other classroom methods.

___ plot summary   ___ review   ___ abstract

3) *Le Morte d'Arthur* is Thomas Malory's early version of the story of King Arthur, of his relations with Queen Guenevere, and of the actions of the knights of the round table, especially Launcelot, Gawain, and Galahad. Although they love their king, both Guenevere and Launcelot are unfaithful. Many knights abandon the kingdom in search of the Holy Grail. Ultimately, the death [*morte*] of Arthur occurs after his own son Mordred betrays him.

___ plot summary   ___review   ___abstract

4) The biography *Oprah Winfrey: Media Success Story* **by Anne Saidman views the life of Winfrey from her childhood days on a farm in Mississippi to her role as talk show host.**

___ plot summary   ___ review   ___ abstract

3c Writing paraphrased note cards

This note is the most difficult to write. It requires you to restate in your own words the thought, meaning, and attitude of someone else. Your task is to interpret and rewrite a source in about the same number of words as the original. Keep in mind these rules for paraphrase:

1) Retain the meaning of the original material in your restatement.

2) Include an in-text citation to the author and page number like this (Jones 193), just as you do for a direct quotation.

3) Rewrite the material in about the same number of words.

4) Put quotation marks around any phrase that you retain from the original.

5) You may and often should credit the source at the beginning of the paraphrase and put the page number at the end. In that way, your reader will know when the paraphrase begins and when it ends.

Note: You can use paraphrase to maintain the sound of

your voice and style as well as to avoid an endless string of direct quotations.

Here are a few examples that show how one writer paraphrased material.

Original: Except for identical twins, each person's heredity is unique.—Fred V. Hein, 294.

Paraphrase: Fred Hein explains that heredity is special and distinct for each of us, unless you are one of identical twins (294).

Original: Since only half of each parent's chromosomes are transmitted to a child and since this half represents a chance selection of those the child could inherit, only twins that develop from a single fertilized egg that splits in two have identical chromosomes.
—Fred Hein, 294

Paraphrase: Twins have identical chromosomes because they grow from one egg that divides after it has been fertilized (Hein 294). Most brothers and sisters differ because of the "chance selection" of chromosomes transmitted by each parent (294).

Original: Adults through the ages have been inclined to judge play to be neither serious nor useful and thus unrelated to the center of human tasks and motives, from which the adult, in fact, seeks "recreation" when he plays.—Erikson, page 18.

Paraphrase: Adults don't think playing has much value, and Erikson says they keep it separated

```
from their work. When adults do play, they call
it "recreation" (18).
```

When readers see an in-text citation but no quotation marks, they will assume that you are paraphrasing, not quoting.

Exercise 3.3 Three paraphrased notes are shown below that are based on an original passage from a book that explains the difference between *play* and *games*. Evaluate each paraphrase.

Original: The essence of *play* is that is has no rules. The essential feature of a *game* is that it involves a formal confrontation between the player and his opponent (or one player in two opposing roles) in which all activity takes place within an agreed system of rules.
—John and Elizabeth Newson, 18.

Now, evaluate each of these paraphrases according to these criteria:

- Retains the meaning of the original material

- Uses new wording

- Cites the original author and page

- Uses quotation marks for any original phrasing.

It seems to me that children left alone have
lots of fun. When a so-called game begins, we
need referees and coaches and rule books.
According to one source, the difference between
merely playing and playing a game is the rules.
The rules seem to establish a "formal
confrontation" (Newson 18).

1. _____	2. _____	3. _____	4. _____
Retains the meaning of the original material	Uses new wording	Cites the original author and page	Uses quotation marks for any original phrasing

When we make up games on the playground, we are
playing and having fun, but when we participate
in little league baseball or soccer, the rules
of the game become very important, so important
in fact that we need referees and rule books and
screaming parents to resolve the formal
confrontations.

1. _____	2. _____	3. _____	4. _____
Retains the meaning of the original material	Uses new wording	Cites the original author and page	Uses quotation marks for any original phrasing

John and Elizabeth Newson explain the difference
between playing for fun and playing a game. They
say that play "has no rules," and they say that
playing a game "involves a formal confrontation"
(18). Maybe that's why the fun disappears when
children get into a little league game dominated
by referees, rules, and screaming parents.

1. _____	2. _____	3. _____	4. _____
Retains the meaning of the original material	Uses new wording	Cites the original author and page	Uses quotation marks for any original phrasing

Exercise 3.4 Below is an original statement about Ernest Hemingway's novel *The Old Man and the Sea*.

Original: The story has been interpreted as a symbolic tale of man's courage and dignity in the face of defeat.
—Philip Young, *World Book Encyclopedia,* H-173

Write a note that *quotes* Philip Young:

Now, write a note that *paraphrases* Philip Young:

3d Understanding primary and secondary sources

Primary sources are the original words of a writer in a novel, poem, play, short story, letter, autobiography, speech, report, film, television program, original design, computer program, interview, and so forth.

Secondary sources are works *about* somebody (biography) or *about* a creative work (critical evaluation). Secondary sources include interpretations of novels or paintings, reviews of plays or movies, or biographies. Other secondary evaluations may appear in news reports, magazine articles, and textbooks.

Think of secondary sources as writing about primary sources and about the creators of primary works. In general, you should paraphrase secondary sources, not quote them, unless the wording of the original is especially well-phrased. However, *do* quote primary sources. Primary Source:

We Real Cool

The Pool Players

Seven at the Golden Shovel

> We real cool. We
> Left school. We
> Lurk late. We
> Strike straight. We
> Sing sin. We
> Thin gin. We
> Jazz June. We
> Die soon.

—Gwendolyn Brooks

from Crossing Cultures, page 155

Secondary Source:

When Gwendolyn Brooks writes about conditions in the black community, her black dialect rings true and her message is filled appropriately with tragic awareness.
—Lawrence Wright from *Modern Poets on the Edge,* page 8.

Student's note using the primary source:

Gwendolyn Brooks has her seven pool players brag. They say "We real cool" and "We Sing sin." But she also shows the bad side of that kind of life, "We Die soon" (155).

Student's note using the secondary source:

One critic says Gwendolyn Brooks does two good things. He says her "black dialect rings true" in "We Real cool" and the poem also shows her "tragic awareness" (Wright 8).

Student's note using both the primary and the secondary sources:

When Gwendolyn Brooks has her seven pool players at the Golden Shovel say, "We real cool," she captures the voice and the attitude of young blacks. When they say, "We Die soon," Brooks shows how they may meet a tragic fate (Wright 8).

Exercise 3.5 Circle below the types of writing that are primary sources:

novel	book review
literary interpretation	play
biography	evaluation of a poem
speech	interview
poem	introduction to a poem
letter	song

3e Altering the sources

You should not copy a secondary source word-for-word unless it is well-worded and all sentences are relevant to your paragraph. Suppose that you have this source:

Acid rain is a popular term for rain, snow, sleet, or other precipitation that has been polluted by such acids as sulfuric acid and nitric acid. These acids are formed when water vapor in the air reacts with certain chemical compounds given off by automobiles, factories, power plants and other sources that burn such fuels as coal, gasoline, and oil. Common acid-forming compounds include sulfur dioxide and nitrogen oxides. In addition, acidic gases and particles in the atmosphere may reach the earth during periods when it is not raining. These dry substances are also significant acid pollutants. Scientists use the term *acid deposition* to refer to both wet and dry acid pollution that falls to the earth.

—Gene E. Likens, *The World Book Encyclopedia,* 1990.

Quote only the part of the source that pertains to your point, not the whole paragraph.

> The average citizen adds to the problem of acid rain by driving an automobile and by heating the home. Sulfuric acid and nitric acid are the enemies. Gene Likens explains:
>
>> These acids are formed when water vapor in the air reacts with certain chemical compounds given off by automobiles, factories, power plants, and other sources that burn such fuels as coal, gasoline, and oil. (A-27)
>
> So each time we turn the ignition switch or turn up the thermostat, we contribute to the growth of acid rain.

Rather than depend heavily on one source, go in search of others and combine them into one paragraph.

> Acid rain is everyone's responsibility. One source explains that acid fallout results from precipitation that has been polluted by sulfur dioxide and nitrogen oxide (Lexicon Webster's Dictionary). Gene Likens explains:
>
>> These acids are formed when water vapor in the air reacts with certain chemical compounds given off by automobiles, factories, power plants, and other sources that burn such fuels as coal, gasoline, and oil. (A-27)

Consequently, all of us add to the problem of acid rain by driving an automobile and by heating the home. At the same time, Christian Mays says that we contribute to the greenhouse effect since acid rain kills the forests. Mays says, "We need the forest to produce carbon dioxide, water vapour, methane, and chlorofluorocarbons" (934). So each time we turn the ignition switch or turn up the thermostat, we contribute to the growth of acid rain.

3f Understanding plagiarism and avoiding it

Plagiarism is the unacknowledged use of another person's work. You cannot present as your own work the words, music, drawings, photographs, or paintings of another person. Plagiarism occurs when you purposely and knowingly commit one of these errors:

- You turn in another student's paper as your own.

- You copy portions of another student's paper into your own.

- You copy source material into your paper without quotation marks and without an in-text citation to author and page.

- You paraphrase source material into your paper without an in-text citation to author and page.

- You summarize source material without a clear

reference to the original source (Note: give author and title but add page numbers only if you are summarizing a specific section of a book.)

Plagiarism violates the academic code of conduct which demands that you must give credit to others for their words and ideas when you use them in your own work. Granted, there are exceptions for common knowledge. Most people know that George Washington was our first president and that he lived at Mount Vernon. However, if one source says Washington often ignored his Secretary of State, Thomas Jefferson, to seek the wisdom of Alexander Hamilton, his Secretary of the Treasury, then a citation to the source would be in order.

Therefore, make it a regular habit to identify the source within your text. When you do, you are adding credibility to your paper. Below is a quotation from a source followed by sample note cards.

Original: Whether they are playing house or dramatizing a far-flung intergalactic adventure, for children, "making believe" is more than just an exercise in imagination—it's learning by doing. During pretend play, children explore and make sense of appropriate and grown-up behaviors, testing their own and others' reactions.
—Helen Boehm, "Toys and Games to Learn By," *Psychology Today* Sept. 1989: 62.

Three of the following note cards demonstrate the proper citation of a source; there is no risk of plagarism in these three. One, however, does not.

During pretend play children
explore grown-up behavior by
playing "doctor" or "astronaut."
Make-believe play is good exercise
for the imagination.

One authority endorses make-believe
play by children who learn from
observing human behavior, their own
and that of others (Boehm 62).

Helen Boehm endorses the role of
make-believe play by children,
saying it is "learning by
doing," as well as "an exercise
in imagination"(62).

"During pretend play," says Helen
Boehm, "children explore and make
sense of appropriate and grown-up
behaviors, testing their own and
others' reactions" (62).

Exercise 3.6 Judge the following notes cards, labeling them *correct* or *incorrect* with regard to proper citation of original information as opposed to common knowledge facts.

Original: Alabama, one of the Southern States, is known as the Heart of Dixie. Alabama occupies a central place in the history of the South. The Constitution of the Confederacy was drawn up in

Montgomery, the state capital. The Alabama Capitol served as the first Confederate Capitol. There, Jefferson Davis took office as President of the Confederacy.

Today, Alabama has a vital part in the nation's future. Huntsville, called *Rocket City, U.S.A.,* is the site of the Redstone Arsenal and the Marshall Space Flight Center. Scientists at Huntsville developed many important rockets and space vehicles, including the Mercury-Redstone rocket system that carried the U.S. astronauts into space.

Most parts of the South did not become widely industrialized until the 1900s. But heavy industry got a relatively early start in Alabama, mainly because of the state's rich mineral resources. Northern Alabama is one of the few areas in the world that has all three main raw materials used in making steel—coal, iron ore, and limestone. Blast furnaces for making iron and steel began operating in Birmingham in the 1880s. After that Birmingham grew rapidly. Today, it is Alabama's largest city.—"Alabama," *World Book,* 1976.

1._____   2._____
Northern Alabama is one   Alabama, called the
of the few areas in the   "Heart of Dixie," has a
world that has all   strong industrial base
three main raw   with Birmingham as the
materials used in   hub.
making steel—coal, iron
ore, and limestone.

3._____

One source says that "heavy industry got a relatively early start in Alabama, mainly because of the state's rich mineral resources" ("Alabama" A-247).

4._____

Most of the South did not become industrialized until late in the 1800s, but Alabama got an early start because of its rich mineral resources used in making steel—coal, iron ore, and limestone ("Alabama" A-247)

5._____

Scientists at Huntsville developed many important rockets and space vehicles, including the Mercury-Redstone rocket system that carried the U. S. astronauts into space.

6._____

While other southern cities failed to attract industry, Birmingham, thanks to vast mineral deposits, developed a large industrial base in the 1880s ("Alabama" A-247).

To avoid plagiarism, you should label note cards carefully to assure yourself that full credit has been given to the sources. Always label your note cards with a descriptive title, list the author, and write down exact page numbers. *Note: The bibliography cards will have full data on the author's work.* Follow the guidelines on the next page for avoiding plagiarism:

Avoiding Plagiarism

1. Introduce the quotation or paraphrase with the name of the authority, or place the name and page number inside the parentheses at the end of the citation.

2. Enclose all direct quotations within quotation marks.

3. Paraphrase material in your own style and language; do not simply rearrange sentence phrases.

4. At the end of each summary, paraphrase, or direct quotation, provide a specific page number within parentheses. If you have not introduced the material with the name of the author, include the name here.

5. For every source mentioned within the paper you must provide a bibliography entry on the "Works Cited" page.

The following sample note cards correctly use direct quotation and paraphrase, and they also demonstrate proper citations to the source.

Original: The car turned off Main Street, the President happy and waving, Jacqueline erect and proud by his side, and Mrs. Connally saying, "You certainly can't say that the people of Dallas haven't given you a nice welcome," and the automobile turning on to Elm Street and down the slope past the Texas School Book Depository, and the shots, faint and frightening, suddenly distinct over the roar of the motorcade, and the quizzical look on the President's face before he pitched over, and Jacqueline crying, "Oh, no, no. . . . Oh, my God, they have shot my husband," and the horror, the vacancy.
—Arthur M. Schlesinger, Jr., A Thousand Days: John F. Kennedy in the White House, 1965, p. 1025.

```
The Last Day              Schlesinger 1025

Kennedy's final moment alive was touched by
deep irony. Immediately prior to the
gunshots, Governor Connally's wife said,
"You certainly can't say that the people of
Dallas haven't given you a nice welcome"
(qtd. in Schlesinger 1025).
```

```
The Last Day              Schlesinger 1025

With his words "the horror, the vacancy,"
Arthur Schlesinger, special assistant to
the President, voiced the private feelings
of John F. Kennedy's staff and the
universal grief of all Americans (1025).
```

Exercise 3.7 Below are the actual words of author Louis L'Amour and the editorial commentary of the Current Biography editors. Judge whether the note cards demonstrate effective use of source materials or demonstrate plagiarism. Label each note as acceptable or plagiarism.

Despite their frequent references to gunplay, intermittent gunfights, and occasional instances of cannibalism, Indian tortures, and hangings, L'Amour's books, compared with those of his rivals, are free of gratuitous violence. L'Amour contends that guns are "over-stressed" in most westerns and likes to remind interviewers that from 1800 to 1816 "there were as many gunfights in our Navy as on the entire frontier." "My whole feeling about the American West, the American frontier, is that a lot more was happening than just a bunch of gunfights or Indian battles," he told Ned Smith. "A lot of cultures were meeting, a lot of influences came together."

—from "Louis L'Amour, *Current Biography Yearbook 1980,* page 205

1._____

L'Amour's books make frequent references to gunplay, to intermittent gunfights, and to Indian tortures, but he doesn't overdo it and argues that more was happening than just a bunch of gunfights or Indian battles.

2._____

"My whole feeling about the American West, the American frontier," says L'Amour, "is that a lot more was happening than just a bunch of gunfights or Indian battles" (qtd. in CB 205).

3._____

One biography argues that L'Amour's fiction, when compared with other westerns, is "free of gratuitous violence," though his writing does have its share of fighting, Indian wars, and occasional hangings (CB 205).

4._____

Louis L"Amour was fascinated by the mix of people and ethnic races on the western frontier. "A lot of cultures were meeting," he said at one point, "a lot of influences came together" (qtd. in CB 205).

5._____

L'Amour contends that guns
are "over-stressed" in most
westerns and likes to
remind interviewers that
from 1800 to 1816 "there
were as many gunfights in
our Navy as on the entire
frontier."

Chapter 4—Outlining

During your early research, you will find certain words and ideas that catch your attention. As soon as you can identify key words, you should draft a preliminary, rough outline. An outline is a list of phrases and sentences to show the shape and boundaries of the paper.

4a Writing a rough outline

A rough outline is your personal guide to the issues raised by your research proposal (see **1c**). It is a tool to help you write about the important ideas. To develop a rough outline, do two things: **1)** jot down key words and phrases for important points, and **2)** arrange the list to separate ideas into main topics and subtopics. Let us suppose that you have written this research proposal:

I want to examine games and toys for their educational value. I may need to warn parents that some claims by toy makers are untrue. Right now, my thesis is something like this—parents need to check with experts in magazines for the best toys, not respond to the labels on the boxes or the TV shows.

Making a rough list

Begin outlining by writing down your key words:

educational toys	girl/boy toys
war toys	preschool toys
computer games that teach	video games

Asking a few questions

This task is more difficult, but it motivates you to begin writing the answers and thereby to start writing portions of your paper.

• Do computer games and video games teach anything worthwhile?
• Are sexist toys discriminatory?
• Do war toys encourage violent behavior?
• Are toy manufacturers a help or a menace to a child's education?

Using the investigative plan

This plan reminds you of your purpose in writing the research paper. It lists the issues and your reasons for writing the paper.

I plan to investigate the following issues:
• preschool toys
• video games that teach
• computer games that teach
• gender-related toys
• war toys
in order to reach a conclusion about the role of educational toys for preschool and kindergarten children.

Ranking your major headings and subheadings

Next, arrange the list into an outline. That is, you will identify the major issues in headlines and then list the supporting ideas as subheads.

```
Educational Toys for School Children

Toys that teach skills
   Electronic toys
      computer games
      video games
      others
   Traditional toys
      puzzles
      blocks, & misc.
Toys as role models
   Girl toys
   Boy toys
Toys that teach social identity
   War toys
   Heroes
   Villains
   Ethnic toys
```

Writing an outline like this one will enable you to arrange your note cards, identify where you need more material, and begin drafting portions of the paper. As you rank your ideas in outline form, you will discover the strengths and weaknesses of your research.

Exercise 4.1 Adjust the following list to rank major issues as headlines and less important ideas as subheads under the appropriate heading.

annoy city dwellers	1. _____
spread seeds	a. _____
helpful birds	b. _____
harmful birds	c. _____
eat orchards	d. _____
eat insects	2. _____
provide fertilizer	a. _____
cause ugly splotches on cars	b. _____
spread diseases	c. _____
eat vineyards	d. _____
offer beauty and music	e. _____

Exercise 4.2 For your own research paper, develop one of the following preliminary steps before writing your outline. You may want to develop all three.

A. List of ideas and issues

Subject_____

Major issues:

1)_____

2)_____

3)_____

4)_____

5)_____

B. A set of questions to be answered

My investigation will search for answers to these questions (consider *why, how, where, what, how much*):

_____

_____

_____

_____

C. An investigative plan

I plan to examine the following issues:

- _____

- _____

- _____

- _____

- _____

in order to reach a conclusion about _____

_____.

Exercise 4.3 After a period of research and note-taking, you need to expand your own outline to rank major ideas and subtopics. Develop your own rough outline below. You need not fill all the blanks; however, under each major heading do try to list at least two subtopics.

_____   _____
 _____   _____
 _____   _____
 _____   _____

 _____   _____
 _____   _____
 _____   _____
 _____   _____

If you cannot list more than one subtopic, look for a
more general headline; your heading may be too
specific.

4b Writing a formal outline

The rough outline will help with your note-taking and
with drafting a few paragraphs. However, you need a
more detailed outline for writing the complete paper. A
formal outline classifies the issues of your study into
clear, logical categories with headings and with one or
more levels of subheadings. Don't think of a formal
outline as rigid and inflexible. You may, and probably
should, modify it while writing your rough draft.

Using standard outline symbols

Formal outlines require a special numbering system, as shown below:

I. ———————————— First major heading

  A. ——————————— Subheading of first degree

    1. ———————— Subheading of second degree

    2. ————————

      a. ——————— Subheading of third degree

      b. ——————

        (1) —————— Subheading of fourth degree

        (2) —————

          (a) ————— Subheading of fifth degree

          (b) ————

  B. ——————————— Subheading of first degree

Using the formal three-part outline

The traditional outline has three sections—introduction, body, and conclusion. The basic model looks like this:

Title

I. Introduction

    A. The background

    B. The problem

    C. The thesis statement

II. Body

    A. First major issue

    B. Second major issue

    C. Third major issue

III. Conclusion

    A. Review of the major issues

    B. The answer, the solution, the final opinion

With this standard plan, you have plenty of freedom to write in your own way. The introduction can include a quotation, an anecdote, a definition, statistics, and other material discussed in Chapter 6. In the body you can compare, analyze, give evidence, trace historical events, and many other things, as explained in Chapter 7.

In the conclusion you can challenge an assumption, take exception to a prevailing point of view, and reaffirm your thesis, as explained in Chapter 8. Note how the following outline adds flesh and bones to the basic model for an introduction:

Advertising in the Schools

I. Introduction
   A. The background
      1. Children with money
         a. Allowances and spending money
         b. Effects on the marketplace
      2. Commercial advertising in schools
         a. Channel One
         b. Educational material from McDonald's
         c. Student clubs selling stuff
   B. The problem
      1. Advertisers in the classroom
         a. Quotation by Carol Herman
         b. Buying classroom time
      2. Money, not the mind of the child, as the target
   C. The thesis statement: School should be a safe zone away from commercials.

Writing a formal outline using topics

You can develop your outline using either phrases or sentences. If you choose a topic outline using phrases, they must be balanced noun phrases (the effects of steroids), gerund phrases *(using* steroids*),* or infinitive phrases *(to use* steroids*).* This example of a topic outline uses noun phrases:

III. The senses
    A. Receptors that detect light
        1. Rods of the retina
        2. Cones of the retina
    B. Receptors that detect vibrations
        1. Outer ear
        2. Middle ear
        3. Inner ear

Here is a brief sample using gerund phrases:

III. Sensing the environment
    A. Detecting light
        1. Sensing dim light with retina rods
        2. Sensing bright light with retina cones

Here is a brief sample using infinitive phrases:

III. To use the senses
    A. To detect light
        1. To sense dim light
        2. To sense bright light

Writing a sentence outline

Rather than write in phrases, you can draft an outline with complete sentences. The sentence outline makes it easy for you to copy the material into your rough draft, thereby speeding the writing process. Note this example:

```
III. The athletes who use steroids get some
increases in their muscles but they also damage
their glands, especially if drug testing doesn't
stop it soon enough.
        A. Athletes and others who use steroids
        get some increases in their muscles and
        impress their coaches who directly or
        indirectly encourage boys and girls to do
        it—"A little more weight, boy, and you'll
        be a starter next year."
            1. Football linemen like extra weight
            so they can stand their ground or
            charge forward to block or to tackle.
            2. Backs can combine steroid use
            with weight programs to develop
            specific leg muscles and thereby
            increase speed and endurance.
        B. Eventually, however, the steroids
        affect the body's glands.
            1. The macho athlete can become sterile.
            2. Damage to the liver and kidneys
            can set in motion an early death.
            3. Heart damage can have an immediate
            effect, during the middle of a game.
```

Writing the sentence outline, like the one shown above, takes more time than the topic outline, but it has the advantage of providing complete ideas when you begin drafting the paper itself.

Exercise 4.4 Write a formal outline for your own paper by filling in the appropriate lines below. You can write either a topic outline (see page 85) or a sentence outline (see page 86). Adjust the outline as necessary to add lines or leave some blank.

Title _____

  I. Introduction

    A. Background

       1. _____

       2. _____

    B. The problem

       1. _____

       2. _____

    C. Thesis sentence: _____

                _____

  II. The Body

    A. Major issue one: _____

       1. _____

       2. _____

    B. Major issue two: _____

       1. _____

       2. _____

    C. Major issue three: _____

       1. _____

       2. _____

  III. Conclusion

    A. Review of the issues

    B. Answer, solution, opinion

Chapter 5—Using In-Text Citations

You will be using references to other
sources throughout your paper. In the
past, footnotes or endnotes were used to
document sources, but current practice
requires what is called *in-text citation* of
each source used in the paper.

In-text citation means that you make reference to your source within the text, not with a raised superscript numeral and a footnote.

This section of the handbook will show you how to write correct in-text citations for many different kinds of sources.

The MLA (Modern Language Association) style requires you to list an author and a page number in your text, usually within parentheses, and then, at the end of your paper, to provide a full bibliography entry on a "Works Cited" page (see Chapter 9).

5a Begin with the author and end with a page number

Introduce a quotation or a paraphrase with the author's name and close it with a page number, placed inside parentheses:

> **Herbert Norfleet states that the use of video games by children improves their hand and eye coordination (45).**

This paraphrase makes absolutely clear to the reader when the borrowed idea begins and when it ends.

Notice how unclear the use of the source can become when the writer does not introduce borrowed material.

A source improperly introduced:

> The use of video games by children improves their hand and eye coordination. Children also exercise their minds by working their way through various puzzles and barriers. "The mental gymnastics of video games and the competition with fellow players are important to young children and their development physically, socially, and mentally" (Norfleet 45).

What was borrowed? It seems that only the final quotation came from Norfleet. Yet in truth the entire paragraph, the paraphrasing and the quotation, came from Norfleet. Norfleet is the expert for this paragraph so the paper should mention his name prominently, as shown below.

A source properly introduced:

> Herbert Norfleet defends the use of video games by children. He says it improves their hand and eye coordination and that it exercises their minds as they work their way through various puzzles and barriers. Norfleet states, "The mental gymnastics of video games and the competition with fellow players are important to young children and their development physically, socially, and mentally" (45).

This paragraph demonstrates correct form:

- It credits the source properly and honestly.

- It shows the correct use of both paraphrase and quotation.

- It demonstrates the student's research into the subject.

An important reason for writing the research paper is to gather and present source material on a topic, so it only follows that you should display those sources prominently in your writing, not hide them or fail to cite them.

Exercise 5.1 The following passage has a citation to name and page at the end of the last sentence, but actually the entire paraphrased passage has been borrowed. Edit it in the margins and between the lines to give credit throughout the paragraph to the original source: Charles R. Larson, *American Indian Fiction,* page 17.

```
There is one story that lies deep in

our reaction to American Indians—

Pocahontas. It is "a living myth that

will not die." But the distortions of
```

```
the Pocahontas myth cause us to

misread and misunderstand subsequent

writings by Indian writers (Larson 17).
```

5b Put the name and page at the end of borrowed material

You can, if you like, put the authority's name and the page number at the end of a quotation or paraphrase, but give your reader a signal to show when the borrowing begins.

```
One source explains that the DNA in the
chromosomes must be copied perfectly during cell
reproduction. "Each DNA strand provides the
pattern of bases for a new strand to form,
resulting in two complete molecules" (Justice,
Moody, and Graves 462).
```

By opening with "One source explains," the writer signals when the borrowing begins.

Exercise 5.2 The following passage cites the authority's name and page only at the end of the passage. The first two sentences are common knowledge, but the final three sentences of the passage were borrowed directly from Robert Barnett. Edit the passage in the margins and between the lines to show when the borrowing begins.

After she learned the concept of

language from Anne Sullivan, Helen

Keller began to develop her amazing

intellect. She learned to speak, and

earned a degree at Radcliffe College

in 1904. Unlocked from her own

handicaps, she began her devoted

efforts to help the blind and other

handicapped persons. She gave frequent

lectures to raise money for the

American Foundation for the Blind.

Later, she donated two million dollars

to establish the Helen Keller

Endowment Fund (Barnett 210).

5c Citing a source when no author is listed

When no author is shown on a title page, cite the title of an article, the name of the magazine, the name of a bulletin or book, or the name of the publishing organization. Note: Look also for the author's name at the bottom of the opening page and at the end of the article.

Citing a title of a report and page number

One bank showed a significant decline in assets despite an increase in its number of depositors (<u>Annual Report</u> 23).

Citing the title of a magazine article and a page number

"In one sense toys serve as a child's tools, and by learning to use the toys the child stimulates physical and mental development" ("Selling" 37).

Note: You should shorten magazine titles to a key word for the citation. You must then give the full title in the "Works Cited" entry (see Chapter 9).

Citing a publisher or corporate body and a page number

The report by the school board endorsed the use
of Channel One in the school system and said
that "students will benefit by the news reports
more than they will be adversely affected by
advertising" (Clarion County School Board 3-4).

Exercise 5.3 How would you write the in-text citation
for this next passage if the information came from page
344 of an unpublished report by Dayton Holding
Company?

One financial institution suggests that each
high school graduate should receive a $10,000
grant that could be used for college, for
starting a business, for savings, or to begin a
marriage on a sound financial basis
(   ).

5d Identifying nonprint sources

On occasion you may need to identify nonprint
sources, such as a speech, the song lyrics from a
compact disk, an interview, or something you have
heard on television. In these cases there will be no
page number, so you can omit the parenthetical

citation. Instead, introduce the nature of the source so that your reader will not expect a page number.

Citing a source that has no page number

Thompson's lecture defined <u>impulse</u> as "an action triggered by the nerves without thought for the consequences."

Mrs. Peggy Meacham said in her phone interview that prejudice against young black women is not as severe as that against young black men.

In his rap song, Julian Young cries out to young people with this message, "Stay in the school, man, stay in the school; learn how to rule, man, learn how to rule."

Exercise 5.4 Write a passage with correct in-text citation to a television program during which a commentator on <u>CBS News</u> said, "The President's policy toward the homeless street people appears nonexistent."

_____

_____

_____

5e Citing somebody quoted in a book or article

Sometimes the writer of a magazine article will quote another person, and you will want to use that same quotation. For example, in a newspaper article in *USA Today,* page 9A, Karen S. Peterson writes this passage in which she quotes two other people:

Sexuality, popularity, and athletic competition will create anxiety for junior high kids and high schoolers, Eileen Shiff says. "Bring up the topics. Don't wait for them to do it; they are nervous and they want to appear cool." Monitor the amount of time high-schoolers spend working for money, she suggests. "Work is important, but school must be the priority."

Parental intervention in a child's school career that worked in junior high may not work in high school, psychiatrist Martin Greenburg adds. "The interventions can be construed by the adolescent as negative, overburdening and interfering with the child's ability to care for himself."

He adds, "Be encouraging, not critical. Criticism can be devastating for the teen-ager."

Suppose that you want to use the quotation above by Martin Greenburg. You will need to cite both Greenburg, the speaker, and Peterson, the person who wrote the article. Note: Peterson's name will appear on a bibliography entry on your "Works Cited" page, but Greenburg's will not because Greenburg is not the author of the article.

Citing a source that another has also cited

After students get beyond middle school, they
begin to resent interference by their parents,
especially in school activities. They need some
space from Mom and Dad. Martin Greenburg says,
"The interventions can be construed by the
adolescent as negative, overburdening and
interfering with the child's ability to care for
himself" (qtd. in Peterson 9A).

As shown above, you need a double reference that
introduces the speaker but that also includes a clear
reference to the book or article where you found the
material. Without the reference to Peterson, nobody
could find the article. Without the reference to
Greenburg, readers would assume that Peterson spoke
the words. If you use a source that paraphases
someone else, use the word *cited* rather than *qtd*.

Exercise 5.5 An author named Shirley Nash wrote an
article on sports medicine in which she quoted a man
named Evans on page 91 and a man named Landover
on page 68. Complete the in-text citations.

Peter Evans condemns any advertising that
"encourages people to overeat and overdrink"
(   ). Even musicians are subject
to sports injuries. Martin Landover says,
"Extended practice sessions as well as the
gyrations on stage can cause serious injury to
musical performers" (   ).

5f Citing material from textbooks and large anthologies

Reproduced below is a small portion of a textbook:

Metaphor

The Skaters

Black swallows swooping or gliding
In a flurry of entangled loops and curves;
The skaters skim over the frozen river.
And the grinding click of their skates, as they impinge
      upon the surface,
Is like the brushing together of thin wing-tips of
      silver.

John Gould Fletcher

—From *Patterns in Literature,* edited by Edmund J.
Farrell, Ouida H. Clapp, and Karen Kuehner, page 814.

If you quote from Fletcher's poem, and if that is all you quote from the anthology, cite the poet and the page number in your text and write a comprehensive entry for the "Works Cited" list.

Name and page number cited in the text:

```
In "The Skaters," John Gould Fletcher compares
"the grinding click" of ice skates to "the
```

brushing together of thin wing-tips of silver"
(814).

Bibliography entry for the "Works Cited" page:

Fletcher, John Gould. "The Skaters."
    Patterns in Literature. Ed. Edmund
    J. Farrell, Ouida H. Clapp, and
    Karen Kuehner. Glenview: Scott,
    1991.

Suppose, however, that you want to quote not only
from Fletcher but also from the authors of the textbook
(Farrell, Clapp, and Kuehner) and from a second poem
in the book by a man named Sarett. Merely make in-
text citations to name and page. Your "Works Cited"
page (see Chapter 9) would then feature a primary
entry to the textbook and various cross references to it,
as shown below.

In the text:

In "The Skaters" John Gould Fletcher compares
"the grinding click" of ice skates to "the
brushing together of thin wing-tips of silver"
(814). The use of metaphor is central to his

poetic efforts. One source emphasizes Fletcher's use of metaphor, especially his comparison of "the silhouettes of a group of graceful skaters to a flock of black swallows" (Farrell et al. 814). Metaphor gives us a fresh look, as when Lew Sarett in his "Requiem for a Modern Croesus" uses coins to make his ironic statement about the wealthy king of sixth century Lydia:

> To him the moon was a silver dollar, spun
> Into the sky by some mysterious
>   hand; the sun
> Was a gleaming golden coin—
>   His to purloin;
> The freshly minted stars were dimes
>   of delight
> Flung out upon the counter of the
>   night.
> In yonder room he lies,
> With pennies in his eye. (814)

Let's suppose that you also cite a portion of *Great Expectations* by Charles Dickens from this same *Patterns* text. Your "Works Cited" page will require four separate entries, mixed by alphabetical order among any other entries. The textbook is cited in full, but the entries to other authors are shortened by cross references (see also Chapter 9, pages 143–152.)

Bibliography entries for the "works cited" page:

Dickens, Charles. <u>Great Expectations</u>. Farrell et
   al. 675-785.

Farrell, Edmund J., Ouida H. Clapp, and Karen
   Kuehner, eds. <u>Patterns in Literature</u>.
   Glenview: Scott, 1991.

Fletcher, John Gould. "The Skaters." Farrell et
   al. 810.

Sarett, Lew. "Requiem for a Modern Croesus."
   Farrell et al. 810.

Note: The reference entry to Farrell et al. is primary; the others make cross references to it. "Et al." is an abbreviation for "and others."

Exercise 5.6 How would you write the in-text citation for the following passage, which was paraphrased from page 101 of *Life Science,* a textbook edited by Balzer et al. and published by Scott, Foresman and Company.

The scientists remind us to admire a red flower
or smell its aroma but also to recognize the
role of specific genes within a chromosome. The
genes carry codes that tell the rose to produce
particular proteins. The gene tells, or codes,
the cells in the petals to be red or codes the
protein to produce a particular smell
   (   ).

5g Adding extra information to in-text citations

As a courtesy to your reader, add extra information within the citation. Show parts of books, different titles by the same writer, or several works by different writers. For example, your reader may have a different anthology than yours, so a reference to *Great Expectations,* Ch. 4, 681, will enable the reader to locate the passage. The same is true with a reference to *Romeo and Juliet* 2.3.65–68. The reader will find the passage in any edition of the play by turning to Act 2, Scene 3, lines 65–68.

Citing one of several volumes

```
In a letter to his Tennessee Volunteers in 1812,
General Jackson chastised the "mutinous and
disorderly conduct" of some of his troops
(Papers 2: 348-49).
```

The citation above gives an abbreviation for the title (*The Papers of Andrew Jackson),* the volume used, and the page numbers.

Citing two or more works by the same author

```
Thomas Hardy reminds readers in his prefaces
that "a novel is an impression, not an argument"
```

and that a novel should be read as "a study of
man's deeds and character" (<u>Tess</u> xxii; <u>Mayor</u> 1).

The writer above makes reference to two different
novels, both abbreviated. Full titles are *Tess of the
D'Urbervilles* and *The Mayor of Casterbridge*.

Abbreviate whenever possible in parenthetical
citations, but not in your text.

Citing several authors who have written on the same topic

Several sources have addressed this aspect of
gang warfare as a fight for survival, not just
for turf (Rollins 34; Templass 561-65; Robertson
98-134).

The citation above refers to three different writers who
treat the same topic.

Exercise 5.7 Use *C* (correct) or *I* (incorrect) to judge
the following sentences for their use of in-text citations.
Keep in mind the lesson on plagiarism (see **3f**, page 66).

Original source: We hold these truths to be self-
evident, that all men are created equal, that they are
endowed by their Creator with certain unalienable
Rights, that among these are Life, Liberty and the

pursuit of Happiness.—Thomas Jefferson, "Declaration of Independence," paragraph 1.

_____ 1. In the "Declaration of Independence" Thomas Jefferson says that "all men are created equal" and that every person has a right to "Life, Liberty and the pursuit of Happiness" (para. 1).

_____ 2. If you accept the point of view that truth is often self-evident, then you must agree that all of us are created equal and therefore have equal rights.

_____ 3. One patriot defended the "unalienable Rights" of Americans to "Life, Liberty and the pursuit of Happiness" (Jefferson para. 1).

Original source: O. Henry's criminal conviction and prison term was for some time the most uncertain and controversial aspect of his life. One of his biographers, Al Jennings, who was in the penitentiary with O. Henry, recounts that the writer's greatest fear was that he would be recognized and greeted by a former inmate while in the company of others. Many of O. Henry's closest acquaintances never knew that he had spent time in prison, and he often juggled dates to account for the years spent in prison.—"O. Henry," *Twentieth-Century Literary Criticism*, 166.

_____ 4. Many people did not know that O. Henry, the famous short story writer, spent time in prison. He carefully juggled dates to account for the years spent in prison.

_____ 5. According to Al Jennings, who spent time in prison with the writer, O. Henry feared that a former inmate might identify him in the presence of friends or relatives (cited in "O. Henry" 166).

_____ 6. One source said that O. Henry juggled dates to account for the years spent in prison ("O. Henry" 166).

_____ 7. A known fact is that O. Henry was a great writer of short stories.

Original source: Communications satellites can be sized and configured in a variety of ways, involving different capacities and power levels, alternate means of on-board propulsion and stabilization, varying useful lifetimes (including the possiblity of manned or unmanned maintenance), adaptation to different boosters, and, for military satellites, incorporation of various survivability measures against hostile environments—George Gerbner, "Communications Satellite," *The Encyclopedia Americana,* 431.

_____ 8. Communications satellites can be sized and configured in a variety of ways, involving different capacities and power levels.

_____ 9. One article explains that communications satellites have various sizes and lifetimes, and engineers can change propulsion, use different boosters, and incorporate military armaments (Gerbner 431).

_____ 10. Communications satellites have various sizes and lifetimes, and engineers can change

```
propulsion, use different boosters, and
incorporate military armaments (from
Encyclopedia Americana page 431).
```

5h Punctuating citations properly and consistently

Keep page citations outside quotation marks but inside the final period (exception: long indented quotations, as shown on pages 108-109). Use no comma between name and page within the citation (Jones 16–17 *not* Jones, 16–17). Do not use *p.* or *pp.* or *page* with the number(s).

Place commas and periods inside quotation marks unless the page citation intervenes. Place semicolons and colons outside the quotation marks.

```
"Modern advertising," says Rachel Murphy, "not
only creates a marketplace, it determines
values." She adds, "I resist the advertiser's
argument that they 'awaken, not create desires'"
(192).
```

The example above shows: **1)** how to interrupt a quotation to insert the speaker, **2)** how to put the comma inside the quotation marks, **3)** how to use single quotation marks within the regular quotation marks, and **4)** how to place the period after a page citation .

When a question mark or an exclamation mark comes at the end of a quotation, keep it inside the quotation mark. Put the citation to the page number(s) up in the text, usually after the name of the source, as shown below:

```
Scientist Jonathan Roberts (54) asks, "Why do we
always assume that bacteria are bad for us?"
```

The example above shows you how to place the page number after the authority's name so that your citation does not interfere with the final question mark. The example below shows you how to place the page citation after a quotation and before a semicolon.

```
Brian Sutton-Smith says, "Adults don't worry
whether their toys are educational" (64); he
adds, "Why should we always put that burden on
the children?"
```

5i Indenting long quotations

Set off long quotations of four or more lines by indenting ten (10) spaces. Do not use quotation marks around the indented material. Place the parenthetical citation after the final period of the quotation, not inside the period.

```
    In his book, A Time to Heal, Gerald Ford,
who replaced Richard Nixon in the White House,
says he was angry and hurt that Nixon had lied
to him, but he was also bothered deeply about
```

Nixon's effect on the status of the Presidency:

> What bothered me most was the nature
> of Nixon's departure. In the 198
> years of the Republic, no President had
> ever resigned, and only one other
> Chief Executive—Andrew Johnson—had
> ever been the target of an
> impeachment effort in the Congress.
> But Nixon, I had to conclude, had
> brought his troubles upon
> himself.(Ford 5)

Exercise 5.8 Judge the punctuation and the use of margins in the following paragraphs and mark each as *C* (correct) or *I* (incorrect). If you mark one as incorrect, edit the passage in the margins and between the lines to correct it.

____ 1. In his book, <u>Blue Highways</u>, William Least Heat Moon describes his three-month travels along the backroads of America. He pictures a typical morning on the road in this way: "Dirty and hard, the morning light could have been old concrete. Twenty-nine degrees inside. I tried to figure a way to drive down the mountain without leaving the sleeping bag. I was stiff—not from the cold so much as from having slept coiled like a grub. Creaking open and pinching toes and fingers to check for frostbite, I counted to ten (twice) before shouting and leaping for my clothes. Shouting distracts the agony." (Moon 118).

_____ 2. During his travels, Moon interviewed various people, including a Hopi Indian named Kendrick Fritz, who said, "To me, being Indian means being responsible to my people. Helping with the best tools. Who invented penicillin doesn't matter" (qtd. in Moon, page 119).

_____ 3. Kendrick Fritz, a Hopi Indian, answered Moon's questions about the Hopi religion by talking of harmony, saying:

> We don't just pray for ourselves, we pray for all things. We're famous for the Snake Dances, but a lot of people don't realize those ceremonies are prayers for rain and crops, prayers for life. We also pray for rain by sitting and thinking about rain. We sit and picture wet things like streams and clouds. It's sitting in pictures. (Qtd. in Moon 121)

_____ 4. Moon asked Kendrick Fritz, "Do you—yourself—think most whites are prejudiced against Indians?" (119). Fritz responded, "About fifty-fifty. Half show contempt because they saw a drunk squaw at the Circle K. Another half think we're noble savages." (Qtd. in Moon 119).

_____ 5. Moon explains in <u>Blue Highways</u> that the Hopi Indian believes in four worlds: a shadowy realm of contentment, a comfortable place of material goods, a time of worry, and a time when selfishness may block the greater vision (122).

Chapter 6—Writing the Introduction

The opening section of your research paper must do more than identify the subject. A good introduction will establish the significance of an issue that warrants the reader's time as well as your efforts in preparing the paper. You should develop the four basic parts of an introduction:

- Identify the subject
- Give background information
- Express the problem
- Provide a thesis statement

By following this plan and by using the techniques described in this chapter, you can develop a complete introduction.

6a Identifying the topic

In writing your introduction, identify your topic as precisely as possible. You can always begin with your thesis sentence, but you may want to try some of the techniques listed below to tell your readers immediately what your subject is.

• Define key terminology so that you and the readers are on common ground.

• Use an anecdote, which is a brief narrative story that shows the subject with action, dialogue, and description.

• Supply data, statistics, and special evidence to show the timely nature of the subject and its significance in our lives.

• Ask a question.

• Relate well-known facts that will appeal to the interests and knowledge of the reader, and then show your special approach.

The following passage opens a research paper with well-known facts, asks a question, and then identifies the topic:

> Children spend money just like adults.
> Individually, we don't have very much, like
> adults do, but we are a big group and we do have
> an effect on the economy. Suppose we all just
> stopped spending money for a week? Somebody
> would notice. Big companies spend millions of

dollars in advertising to reach us, and the
advertising always finds new ways to get our
money. Now companies are coming into school
buildings with give-aways that carry their logos
and their ads.

The next opening begins with an anecdote, then shifts
to the topic and the thesis sentence:

I work part-time at a local retail store.
One day, while I was behind the counter near the
cash register, I watched a nice-looking woman
browse through the aisles. Every once in a while
she would stuff merchandise into her large
handbag—a blouse, pantyhose, and several pieces
of cheap costume jewelry. She was a shoplifter!
But I've learned she's just one among many.
Shoplifters cause stores to raise their prices
to offset theft losses and the cost of security.
Just as bad, this woman, who was caught red-
handed, managed to have the case dismissed. I
saw her again yesterday, roaming about the mall.

6b Providing background information

In providing background information in your
introduction, you may need to trace the historical
nature of your topic, give biographical data on a
person, or provide general evidence. You may want to
offer a brief summary of a novel, long poem, or other
work to refresh the reader's memory about details of

plot, character, and so forth. Or, you may supply a quotation by an authority to show the importance of the subject. The example below includes background information, a quotation, and ends with a thesis sentence:

> Today's advertisers have breached a
> sanctuary—the school classroom. Channel One not
> only brings a daily news program into the
> schools but also a set of commercials. Teachers
> distribute free educational materials that bear
> the logos of McDonald's, Nutrasweet, Chef
> Boyardee, and others. Student clubs must sell
> products to raise funds. Advertising executive
> Carol Herman puts it bluntly:
>
>> It isn't enough to just advertise on
>> television. . . . You've got to reach
>> kids throughout the day—in school, as
>> they're shopping in the mall . . . or
>> at the movies. You've got to become part
>> of the fabric of their lives. (Qtd. in
>> "Selling" 518)
>
> In effect, advertisers have bought their way
> into the classroom with free educational
> materials, but the target is the dollar bill of
> the child, not the mind of the child.

The next sample provides some general background information on the author, a summary of the short story, and a quotation from the story:

> Louis L'Amour is a famous writer of western
> stories such as <u>Hondo</u>, <u>The Daybreakers</u>, and <u>The
> Lonesome Gods</u>. According to one source, more

than one hundred thirty million copies of his
books have been sold (Farrell et al. 429). His
"War Party" tells the story of Bud, a teenager
who must become a man overnight after his dad
gets killed by Indians. Both Bud and his mother
demonstrate their courage by facing up to the
Indians as well as enduring jealous envy by
their fellow travelers. L'Amour describes the
western frontier in this way:

> When a body crossed the Mississippi
> and left the settlements behind,
> something happened to him. The world
> seemed to bust wide open, and
> suddenly the horizons spread out and
> a man wasn't cramped anymore. The
> pinched-up villages and the
> narrowness of towns, all that was
> gone. The horizons simply exploded
> and rolled back into enormous
> distance, with nothing around but
> prairie and sky. (418-19)

6c Establishing the problem

You can establish the problem to be explored in your
paper by stating one issue that you want to examine. It
can be a question, an assertion, a denial, an
assumption, or a challenge to existing conditions.

Why do schools need dress codes? Nothing is
gained by them. Students who want to show off
will do so anyway.

It can raise both positive and negative issues, which means you compare and contrast the negative forces in light of the positive.

Although Bud is the narrator and principle character in L'Amour's "War Party," the mother is the one who demonstrates great strength of character.

You might even take exception to a prevailing point of view or challenge an assumption so that readers will recognize your perspective, your argument, or your contention.

People who say standard English is the norm for those who expect success forget that most Hispanics don't understand the Gringo meaning of "success." Law school? Dental school? There's no such dream in this world.

In the following opening, the writer begins with the thesis sentence, provides a quotation, offers evidence, and ends by establishing the problem.

Shoplifting in stores all over America has reached the point that all shoppers are suspects; each of us are photographed, followed, watched. Susan Schneider says, "The assumption is that there are no honest shoppers" (38). And what's worse, the people who use the "five-finger discount" come from all walks of life—the unemployed, sure, but also doctors, lawyers, wealthy matrons, congressmen, and even the mayor of a large city. As a result, the clerks in many retail stores look at us, especially teenagers, with ill-will, not friendliness, and treat us with suspicion, not trust.

6d Expressing a thesis sentence in the opening

At some point in the introduction, you need to state your thesis sentence. The usual place is at the end of the introduction, but it can appear almost anyplace. (See pages 17–18 for additional discussion of the thesis sentence.) Remember, the thesis sentence states your convictions about the topic, advances your position, and limits the scope of the study. It must advance your theory about the issue and invite the reader into the argument. Here are two examples:

Advertisers have bought their way into the classroom with free educational material, but their target doesn't seem to be the mind of the child. Their target is the dollar bill in Susie's purse and the quarters clutched in Otis's hand.

"War Party" is not Bud's story, although he tells it. The true heroine is Bud's mother, who stands up to the men on the wagon train and who faces up bravely to the Sioux.

Exercise 6.1 In the margin on the left side, identify the parts of the following introduction. Locate the thesis,

thesis, the assertion of a problem, the identification of the topic, the background information. Is there a summary, evidence, a quotation?

Louis L'Amour is a famous writer of western stories such as Hondo, The Daybreakers, and The Lonesome Gods. According to one source, more than one hundred thirty million copies of his books have been sold (Farrell et al. 429). His story "War Party" tells the story of Bud, a teenager who must become a man overnight after his dad gets killed by Indians. Both Bud and his mother demonstrate their courage by facing up to the Indians as well as enduring jealous envy by their fellow travelers. L'Amour describes the western frontier in this way:

> When a body crossed the Mississippi and left the settlements behind, something happened to him. The world seemed to bust wide open, and suddenly the horizons spread out and a man wasn't cramped anymore. The pinched-up villages and the narrowness of towns, all that was gone. The horizons simply exploded and rolled back into enormous distance, with nothing around but prairie and sky. (418-419)

People had to grow up fast on the frontier. Although Bud is the narrator and principal character, the mother is the one who demonstrates great strength. So "War Party" is not Bud's story, although he tells it. The true heroine is Bud's mother who stands up to the men on the wagon train and who faces up bravely to the Sioux chief.

Exercise 6.2 In the spaces below, begin sketching your own introduction. Try to fill each section.

Identify the topic

_____

_____

Provide some background information

_____

_____

_____

_____

Furnish a good quotation from the sources

_____

_____

_____

Express the problem

_____

_____

_____

State your thesis sentence

_____

_____

_____

Chapter 7—Writing the Body

The body should develop the major issues of your outline. The body should explore at least two major issues, but you may have three, even four or more. That is, it should identify your major areas of interest and explore each one with a variety of techniques, as explained in this chapter.

Here is a sample plan for one student's paper on Martin Luther King, Jr. The writer used it as a framework for the body of her paper.

II. The Body

   A. Major issue one: *Civil Rights Movement*

     1. *successful leadership of "Montgomery Bus Boycott"*

     2. *speech called "I Have a Dream"*

   B. Major issue two: *preoccupation with death*

     1. *deep apprehensions about going to Washington*

     2. *his speech made on April 3*

   C. Major issue three: *commitment to his cause*

     1. *poor people's campaign (danger of it)*

     2. *arrested and jailed several times during protest*

This plan enabled the writer to develop several paragraphs on the key discoveries of her investigation. The material supported her introduction and pointed forward to her conclusion. You can add substance to the body of your paper by using several strategies, as explained in Section **7a**.

7a Using writing strategies to build the body

As with the introduction, you should pick and choose your techniques. Some techniques will trace the issues and events, others will compare, and still others will classify and analyze.

Chronology

Use **chronology** to trace historical events and to explain a sequence by time. You may need to discuss the causes or consequences of certain events.

> Gaining courage and strength to face the frontier is not an overnight affair. Bud and his mother in L'Amour's "War Party" cross the Mississippi and enter areas where "the horizons simply exploded and rolled back into enormous distance, with nothing around but prairie and sky" (419). Life will not be easy and they will face many hardships. Early on, the Indians kill Bud's father, but Bud and his mother push forward.

Keep the plot summary short and relate it to your thesis, as shown by the first sentence of the passage above. Do not allow plot summary to extend beyond one paragraph; otherwise, you may retell the entire story. Your task is to make a point, not retell the story.

Comparison and contrast

Employ **comparison** and **contrast** to show the two sides of a subject, to compare two characters, to contrast the past with the present, or to examine positive and negative issues.

> Bud is still a child, but he is tough and smart. He kills a buffalo, and later on he kills an antelope on the run. He knows when to remain silent and when to speak out boldly. However, his mother is the heroine of the story. She is the one who decides to continue west after her husband, Bud's father, has been killed. In fact, she killed the Indian who sent the fatal arrow into her husband. She faces up to Mr. Buchanan, who wanted her to turn back. She confronts the Sioux chief. She ignores the grumbling of fellow travelers. She makes a home.

Cause and effect

Write **cause** and **effect** to develop the reasons for a circumstance and/or to examine the consequences.

> Sometimes a child is only as strong as adults will allow. In "War Party" Bud rises to a new level because his mother lets it happen. She tells Buchanan, "I have my man. Bud is almost thirteen and accepts responsibility. I could ask for no better man" (420). Bud rewards her confidence at the end of the story by

confronting Buchanan: "Mr.Buchanan, I may be little and may be a fool, be this here rifle doesn't care who pulls its trigger" (427).

Classify and analyze

Classify and **analyze** the various issues. Spend some time discussing the various items to develop each one as evidence in support of the thesis sentence.

Was Bud's mother in "War Party" a Sioux Indian? She spoke the language and was able to calm the Sioux chief and his braves. In truth, she saved the wagon train. But the people were suspicious. How did she know the Sioux language? Some of them wanted to kick her off the wagon train because she was surely a squaw. As it turned out, she was not an Indian at all. She had grown up playing with Sioux youngsters in Minnesota. At a crucial moment, she drew upon that knowledge to save her family.

Developing a paragraph or two on each method of development is one way to build the body of your paper. Write a comparison paragraph, then classify and analyze one or two issues, then pose a question and answer it. Sooner than you think, you will draft the body of the paper.

Definition

Use **definition** to expand upon a complex subject.

> For some people the frontier of the American west was an opportunity, for some it was challenge, and for others it was dangerous territory best avoided. To Bud in "War Party" the frontier was adventure. To his mother it would be "home." Bud thought home was something they had left. His mother explained, "Home is where we're going now, and we'll know it when we find it" (420). Bud accepted her definition, but he also said:
>
>> She might tell us that home was where we were going, but I knew home was where ma was, a warm and friendly place with biscuits on the table and fresh-made butter. We wouldn't have a real home until ma was there and we had a fire going. Only I'd build the fire. (420)

Process analysis

A **process analysis** paragraph is useful in explaining the steps necessary to achieve a desired end.

> For the frontier hero, the first step is making the decision to cross the Mississippi. The second stage is finding the courage to continue the quest against boredom, danger, poor

weather, and lack of supplies. The third stage
is overcoming the fear of death by accident,
drowning, trampling, or the Indians. The fourth
stage, and the most dangerous, is facing the
envy and jealousy of companions and fellow
travelers.

Question and answer

You can also present information by framing a
question, and then **answering** it with specific details
and evidence.

> Were early frontiersmen prejudiced in their
> treatment of women? L'Amour's story gives up a
> loud "yes." One of the rules of the wagon train
> demonstrates the prejudice: "There has to be a
> man with every wagon" (420). A few travelers
> condemned her for her outspoken ways and her
> determination to continue west without her
> husband. Later, when she confronted the Sioux
> chief, many people thought she was out of place,
> that confronting an Indian was a man's job. They
> even suspected that Mrs. Miles was an Indian herself.

Evidence from source material

Cite the various **authorities** on the subject. Provide
quotations, paraphrases, and summaries in support of
your topic sentences.

Louis L'Amour came by his knowledge from people who lived the frontier life, including one old man who had been a captive of the Apaches and raised in his childhood with them (_CB_ 203). Having used the old man as a reference source, L'Amour says, "He was a man who knew all about the Apaches, how they lived, how they worked, how they fought" (qtd. in _CB_ 203). L'Amour adds, "In much of his thinking, he was still an Apache."

There is no reason to provide a page citation for the final quotation because it obviously came from the same source.

Cite every source, but do not needlessly clutter your text with citations when the reference is clear to the reader.

Note: There are several other methods for developing paragraphs: description, statistics, symbolism, point of view, scientific evidence, history, character, setting, and others.

7b Writing effective topic sentences

Paragraphs of a research paper need substance. Your topic sentence sets the stage for full development of ideas and issues. Here are a few suggestions.

1) Write a topic sentence that requires you to classify and explain several stages of development.

```
There are four stages to the creation of acid
rain.
The pageantry of high school football includes
far more than the game itself.
Several theories exist about the extinction of
the giant dinosaurs.
```

2) Use a question as the topic sentence.

```
What is acid rain?
How does the average citizen contribute to the
build-up of acid rain?
```

3) Write a topic sentence that allows you to expand with chronological information.

```
Most amphibians experience a metamorphosis (a
change in their bodies) as they grow and
develop.
```

4) Write a topic sentence that allows you to expand with description.

```
The turtle's shell is a burdensome shield.
```

5) Write a topic sentence that challenges an assumption and thereby requires a well-developed defense.

```
The year 1991 was not merely the year of Desert
Storm.
```

6) Write a topic sentence that introduces the scholarship on the subject.

```
Several critics have examined Hawthorne's
imagery of darkness and gloom.
```

7) Write a topic sentence that is broad enough to demand specific information.

```
Humans as well as animals learn by association.
```

Topic sentence #7 is printed again below, followed by a paragraph that develops it. Notice how this topic sentence invites readers into a discussion of learning and the paragraph follows with examples of both human and animal behavior.

```
     Humans as well as animals learn by
association. We respond in a predictable pattern
to a certain stimulus. A cat hears the electric
can opener and comes running to the kitchen,
expecting to be fed. A basketball player hears a
referee's whistle and groans, expecting to be
called for committing a foul. We learn by
associating the sound to a specific result. "One
kind of learning by association results in
conditioned response—a desired response to an
unusual stimulus" (Balzar et al. 368). Pavlov's
experiments many years ago proved that dogs
could learn a conditioned response. We also
learn by positive reinforcement and by rewards,
as demonstrated by well-behaved children just
before Christmas or by performing bears at a
circus.
```

7c Writing paragraphs of substance

Give readers sufficient evidence to support each topic sentence. The paragraphs in the body of the research paper ought to be at least one-half page in length. You can do this only by writing good topic sentences and by developing them with the techniques explained above.

> If shoplifters with sticky fingers are looting retail stores in ever larger numbers, a simple question is this one: Who pays? Well, the bill comes to you and me, the honest shoppers who must make up the difference. And we have to pay not only for shoplifting but also for the cost of security measures. Jack Fraser, a retail executive, states: "Stores are losing 1.94 percent of sales per year—and that doesn't even include the expense of maintaining the security staff and equipment. That's a lot of cash. It cuts into profits" (qtd. in Schneider 38).

This writer uses a question-and-answer sequence to build the paragraph by posing the question, "Who pays?" The writer then answers it, "consumers pay," and she defends that answer with a quotation from an authority on the subject.

Almost every paragraph you write in the body of the research paper is, in one way or another, explanatory. You must state your position in a good topic sentence and then list and evaluate your evidence.

Notice how the following writer defends her topic sentence with specific details. The accumulation of evidence builds a paragraph of substance.

Let the real world into the public schools. Channel One furnishes a satellite dish for every school and a television set for every classroom. We should use them. They bring PBS programs and other news and features to the students. We should use videotapes, cam-recorders, audio cassettes with "walkmen," electronic keyboards, computers. Some students have better electronic equipment at home in their bedrooms than in their schools. A teacher, a desk, and a book can't cut it anymore. The Apple Corporation has made gifts of computers to schools for many years now. They had a profit motive, but so what? Look at the tradeoff. Worse, look at the alternative—no computers at all in the schools.

Exercise 7.1 Rather than merely writing a paragraph as it occurs to you, take time to list the technique(s) that you could use to build the paragraph. A paragraph plan reads like this:

I'm going to list the Tennessee battles of General Ulysses Grant to show his progressive fulfillment of a major plan. The paragraph will help defend the topic sentence about Grant as both a patient and a determined commander.

I'm going to classify certain educational toys for preschool children to examine and evaluate their effectiveness in later paragraphs.

Use the space below to tell about the technique(s) you will use for developing one paragraph of your body:

I'm going to _____

_____

_____

_____

_____

Exercise 7.2 Use the space below to write a paragraph of your paper.

_____

_____

_____

_____

_____

_____

_____

_____

_____

_____

_____

_____

Chapter 8—Writing the Conclusion

The conclusion of a research paper
reaffirms the thesis sentence, discusses
the issues, and reaches a final judgment.
The conclusion is not a summary; it is a
belief based on your reasoning and on the
evidence you have accumulated. This is
the place to share with readers the
conclusions you have reached because
of your research.

8a Writing a fully developed conclusion

The nature of the study can dictate your use of the following items in your conclusion. Use several of the techniques to build a conclusion of substance.

1) Reaffirm the topic and restate your thesis to express your primary ideas.

> Shoplifting by a few people casts a shadow on every man, woman, and child who enters a retail store. In a small convenience store as well as a huge department store every person is a potential customer. Unfortunately, every customer is also a potential shoplifter in the eyes of the clerks. You and me—we are suspects no matter how noble we may be.

2) Supply a quotation or two in defense of your position.

> Schneider says, "While the incidence of other larcenies has dropped, the FBI reported that shoplifting rose 33 percent between 1985 and 1989 and that about a million shoplifters are arrested every year" (39). And the evidence gets more persuasive. Schneider adds, "For every person who gets caught, ten get away" (19).

3) Conclude with an anecdote, which is a brief narrative story that will show the subject with action, dialogue, and description.

Jeremy Thorton, who operates a small neighborhood grocery store, relates one of his experiences:

> I caught a 10-year-old girl putting candy inside her dress. What to do? She denied it, and I can't search her. So I let her go. Ten minutes later her mother comes in, busts me in the mouth, and calls me a dirty old man. I'm only 45, but I'm ready to lock the doors and retire. (Qtd. in Rover 34–35)

No wonder owners and store clerks like Thorton view every shopper with suspicion, not trust, and at times with open hostility rather than old fashioned courtesy.

4) Take exception to a prevailing point of view or challenge an assumption so that readers will recognize your perspective, your argument, your contention.

Like other people, I resent being treated as a thief, being televised, watched, and forced to walk through detectors when I leave a store. But after investigating the facts, I understand why.

5) Discuss the data, statistics, and special evidence to show their relevance to your final statements.

Jack Fraser, a retail executive, states: "Stores are losing 1.94 percent of sales per year—and that doesn't even include the expense of maintaining the security staff and equipment" (qtd. in Schneider 38).

6) Compare past events to the present situation, compare prior findings to the present evidence, or compare outdated ideas in light of contemporary thinking.

```
Burglary during hours when retail stores are
closed is minor in comparison with shoplifting
thefts when stores are open. Amazing as it
seems, thieves would rather operate during
daylight hours than break into the store at
night.
```

7) Focus on the central figure to discuss the contributions made by a novelist, a political figure, a military hero, and so forth. Use this technique with biography and with literary studies.

```
    L'Amour is noted as a writer of the western
frontier, and people probably think of him as a
rugged male who has little use for women, rather
like Mr. Buchanan in "War Party." But L'Amour
demonstrates a pretty good understanding of
women. He shows that they can be tough if
necessary and that they have visions for the
future. Mrs. Miles is not a feminist by modern
standards, but she holds her own in a man's
world.
```

Exercise 8.1 In the space of the left margin identify these techniques used in developing the conclusion: **1)** reaffirms the topic, **2)** uses a quotation from the sources, **3)** takes exception to a prevailing point of view and challenges an assumption, **4)** uses a question and answer sequence, **5)** cites facts and evidence, and **6)** reaches a final judgment.

_____

Maybe the issue of advertising in the classroom is not too important. Many students seem to enjoy the benefits of educational packages, such as Channel One or McDonald's school magazine. But

_____

the evidence suggests something different. Today's students are overweight because of poor diets, they are overly violent because of the media influences, they smoke deadly cigarettes, and they drink excessively in comparison

_____

with previous generations. Can we blame advertising and the companies behind the products? Yes, I think so. The Consumer's

_____

Union says, "We believe promotions that target children should be held to higher standards than those aimed at adults" ("Selling" 521). Teachers

_____

should screen advertising in the classroom. The school should not seem to be endorsing any products.

8b Writing conclusions that have substance

In your conclusion, try to carry your reader to a new level of perception about the topic. A summary of what you have said in the paper is not satisfactory. After all, the reader will hardly need reminding of things just read. Therefore, use a combination of the techniques explained in **8a.**

Notice the manner in which the following conclusion uses these techniques: reaffirms the topic and thesis, cites specific facts, uses a paraphrase from an authority, challenges an assumption, compares outdated ideas in light of contemporary thinking, and reaches a final conclusion.

> Commercial advertising in the classroom poses a danger only if cigarettes and other harmful products are bought and used by the students. At the moment, when funds are low, teachers should use free educational packages from McDonald's, Channel One, Apple, and other companies. School officials get too serious. Malcolm Watson, a psychologist, says young people use play to work out problems or troubling situations (cited in Kantrowitz 72). So let us work a mathematics game on an Apple computer, do an art assignment with <u>MacPaint,</u> or learn the vocabulary using <u>Word Attack</u>. Maybe we don't need spin-the-bottle in the classroom, but it would certainly teach us things about human relations. The electronic age is here now, and classrooms cannot be isolated from video, radio,

cassettes, computers, and so forth. Finally, let's remember the teachers. They can control the effects of advertising in the schools, and the lesson we learn will help us face network television when we get home.

Exercise 8.2 Plan your own conclusion. In the spaces provided below, describe the methods that might help you write an effective conclusion. An example follows:

My conclusion about teenage suicide will do these things: restate my thesis, quote George Goodwin and take exception to his point of view, cite again my collected evidence from personal interviews, and end with the final moments of one teenager's losing struggle to be heard.

My conclusion about _____ will do these things:

_____

_____

_____

_____

_____

_____

_____

Exercise 8.3 Begin drafting your own conclusion by making notes in the spaces below, as appropriate to your subject. Remember to share with the reader your final judgment about the subject; avoid simply repeating what you have already said in the introduction or the body.

_____

_____

_____

_____

_____

_____

_____

_____

_____

_____

_____

Chapter 9—Works Cited

The "Works Cited" page is a bibliography
of the sources you cited in your paper.
A bibliography is a list of books and
articles about a particular subject. The
bibliography serves others who might
wish to read further in the literature.

9a Writing bibliography entries for books

In preparing this page, align the first line of each source with the left margin and indent succeeding lines five spaces. Double-space throughout. Do not list sources that you skimmed but did not use in the paper. Use the following examples as models.

Use this order: author(s), title, a specific volume number, editor(s), edition other than the first, number of volumes if more than one, place and date of publication, publisher (abbreviated), section and page. List the items that your reader might need to find the source.

Abbreviate the names of the publishers. Use this list as a guide:

Scott (Scott, Foresman and Company)
Norton (W. W. Norton and Company)
Allyn (Allyn and Bacon, Inc.)
Bobbs (Bobbs-Merrill Co., Inc.)
Holt (Holt, Rinehart, and Winston, Inc.)
Oxford UP (Oxford University Press)
U of Chicago P (University of Chicago Press)

Book: One author

Zindel, Paul. <u>The Pigman</u>. New York:
     Bantam, 1978.

Book: Two authors, edition other than the first

Bining, Arthur C., and Thomas C.
    Cochran. <u>The Rise of American
    Economic Life</u>. 4th ed. New York:
    Scribner's, 1964.

Book: Anthology, textbook, other edited works

Magill, Frank N., ed. <u>Masterpieces of
    World Literature</u>. New York: Harper,
    1989.

Farrell, Edmund J., Ouida H. Clapp, and
    Karen J. Kuehner, eds. <u>Patterns in
    Literature</u>. Glenview: Scott, 1991.

If you cite one work from an anthology, use this form:

Keats, John. "Ode to a Nightingale."
    <u>Literature of the Western World</u>. Ed.
    Brian Wilkie and James Hurt. 2nd ed.
    2 vols. New York: Macmillan, 1988.
    II: 787-99.

However, if you cite several individual authors from one anthology, you will need a primary reference to the text and several cross references to it (see also pages 99–104.).

Keats, John. "Ode to a Nightingale."
    Wilkie and Hurt, II: 797-99.

Homer. The Odyssey. Wilkie and Hurt, I:
    254–573.

Wilkie, Brian, and James Hurt, eds.
    Literature of the Western World. 2nd
    ed. 2 vols. New York: Macmillan,
    1988.

Wolfe, Thomas. "An Angel on the Porch."
    Wilkie and Hurt, II: 1291–96.

Book: Part of one volume with page numbers

Seale, William. The President's House:
    A History. 2 vols. Washington: White
    House Historical Assn., 1986. II:
    915–1001.

Book: One volume of several volumes

Jackson, Andrew. The Papers of Andrew
    Jackson: 1770–1803. Vol. 1. Ed. Sam
    B. Smith and Harriet C. Owsley. 4
    vols. Knoxville: U of Tennessee P, 1980.

Book: A novel in a special edition

Hardy, Thomas. <u>The Mayor of</u>
    <u>Casterbridge</u>. A Norton Critical
    Edition. Ed. James K. Robinson. New
    York: Norton, 1977.

Book: Two works by the same author

Dickens, Charles. <u>David Copperfield</u>. A
    Norton Critical Edition. Ed. James
    K. Robinson. New York: Norton, 1977.

---. <u>Hard Times</u>. New York: Macmillan, 1962.

Note: Use three dashes, not three underline marks.

9b Writing bibliography entries for magazines, journals, and newspapers

Magazines

Use this order: author(s), title of the article within
quotation marks, name of the magazine underlined,
specific date, inclusive page numbers (but use a "+"

with the opening page if advertising pages intervene or if the article skips to the back pages of the magazine, for example 14+).

Magazine: One author

Schneider, Susan. "The Trade in Sticky
    Fingers." <u>Lear's</u> September 1990: 38+.

Magazine: Two authors

Johnson, Lorenzo, and Peggy L.
    Forrester. "Toys That Teach." <u>Games</u>
    16 April 1990: 34-37.

Magazine: No author listed

"Selling to Children." <u>Consumer Reports</u>
    55 Aug. 1990: 518-21.

Note: this magazine publishes with continuous pagination for the whole year; it requires a volume number, like a journal article (see next page).

Magazine: Review article

Provide reviewer and title of the review as well as the work and author under review.

Beeston, Richard. "Book Reviews." Rev.
of <u>A Touch of Genius: The Life of T.
E. Lawrence</u>, by Malcolm Brown and
Julia Cave. <u>Smithsonian</u> July 1990:132-33.

Journals

Most journals page continuously through all issues of an entire year. Thus the volume number, year (in parentheses), and pages are sufficient for locating a journal article. If a journal does page anew, provide the issue number (for example, "66.2")

Tegano, Deborah, Janet K. Sawyers, and
James D. Moran. "Problem-Finding and
Solving in Play: The Teacher's
Role." <u>Child Education</u> 66 (1989):92-97.

Newspapers

Include the section with the page number.

Hellmich, Nanci. "College Studies Are
Often a Full-time Job." <u>USA Today</u> 11
Sept. 1990: 1D.

9c Writing bibliography entries for other types of sources

Conform to the examples below for entries to a government document, a bulletin, cassette tape, computer data, film, interview, letter, microfilm, music, television, videotape, and so forth. Provide enough information so that readers can understand exactly the nature of the source.

Government documents

Provide government, body, subsidiary body, title, identifying numbers, publication facts.

```
United States. Cong. Senate. Anti-Flag
     Desecration. S. 607 to accompany
     S.R. 412. 102nd Cong., 1st sess.
     Washington: GPO, 1990.
```

Bulletins

```
Alexander, Ralph. Sports and Steroids.
     Bulletin 24A. Washington, DC: GPO, 1989.
```

Cassette tapes

Burney, Elizabeth C. "Comic Women in
    Shakespeare." Lecture on cassette
    tape. Nashville: Vanderbilt U, 1991.

Magazine advertising

"Mexico World Environment Day."
    Advertising page. <u>Smithsonian</u> July
    1990:143.

Computer handbooks

<u>Wordstar Reference</u>. Computer software.
    Novato, CA: Wordstar International, 1990.

Electronic sources

New technology makes it possible for you to have
access to 100 or more books on one compact disk.
You can copy sections of these books onto
your floppy disk or to a hard disk, and then
you can incorporate the material into your
paper without having to retype the
information. However, you must cite the electronic
source you have used.

CD-ROM

The Bible. CD-ROM Dataset—The Old
     Testament. Parsippany, NJ: Bureau
     Development, 1990.

Shakespeare, William. Hamlet.
     Shakespeare on CD-ROM. N.p.: CMC
     Research, 1989.

*Note: "N.p." indicates that the researcher could not
locate a place of publication.*

Williams, T. Harry. The Military
     Leadership of the North and South.
     1960. US History on CD-ROM.
     Parsippany, NJ: Bureau Development, 1990.

Data base sources

"Alexander Hamilton." Academic
     American Encyclopedia. 1981 ed.
     CompuServe, 1983, record no. 1816.

Nevin, John J. "Doorstop to Free
     Trade." Harvard Business Review 61
     (1983): 88-95. DIALOG Information
     Services, 1983, record no. 83-N43.

Television or radio programs

The Commanders: Douglas MacArthur. New
     York: NBC-TV, 17 Mar. 1975.

Shakespeare, William. <u>As You Like It</u>.
    Nashville: Nashville Theatre
    Academy, WDCN-TV, 11 Mar. 1975.

Videotape

Thompson, Paul. "W.B.Yeats." Lecture on
    Videotape. VHS-MSU 160. Memphis:
    Memphis State U, 1982.

Sevareid, Eric. <u>CBS News</u>. New York:
    CBS-TV, 11 Mar. 1975; Media Services
    Videotape 1975-142. Nashville:
    Vanderbilt U, 1975.

Interview

Norfleet, Joe Eddie. Interview with the
    county historian. Dalton, GA 6 July
    1990.

Letters

Wilfong, Richard, and Wynona Wilfong.
    Letter to the author. 14 Mar. 1990.

Maps

Clayton County Topography. United
    States Base Map GA-56, No. 19.
    Washington, DC: GPO, 1985.

Exercise 9.1 The following numbered items have scrambled information to books, magazines, and other sources. Write a correct bibliography entry for each one.

1) Interview. April 5, 1991. Dayton, Ohio. Jane Pullet, county historian.

_____

_____

2) *Encyclopedia Americana.* "Communication Satellite." 1988 edition.

_____

_____

3) *USA Today.* Mary Beth Marklein, author. "Colleges Help Newcomers Find the Way." Wednesday, September 19, 1990, page 9A.

_____

_____

4) *Three Famous Short Novels* by William Faulkner published in 1942 by Vintage Books in New York.

_____

_____

5) *Correspondence of Andrew Jackson* by Andrew Jackson. Volume 1 of 2 volumes. Edited by J. S. Bassett. Published in Washington, D. C., by Carnegie Institution of Washington, 1926.

9d A sample "Works Cited" page

A final "Works Cited" page must list each source that you cite in your text, and only those sources. If you list sources that you did not cite in the text, call the list "References." If you use nonprint sources, label the list "Sources Cited." Your working bibliography cards (see Chapter 2) will provide the basis for your list if you have kept the cards up-to-date. Arrange the list in alphabetical order by the last name of the author. Double-space throughout. If no author is listed, alphabetize by the first important word of the title. If an author has two works, substitute three dashes for the name (see the following page). If you make cross references to an anthology, mingle the references alphabetically with the other entries.

Works Cited

Allison, John. "The Mero District."
    American Historical Magazine 50.2
    (1896): n.p.

Curtis, James C. _Andrew Jackson and the_
    Search for Vindication. Boston:
    Little, 1976.

Durham, Walter T. _The Great Leap_
    Westward: A History of Sumner
    County, Tennessee. Gallatin, TN:
    Sumner County Public Library Board,
    1969.

---. _James Winchester: Tennessee_
    Pioneer. Gallatin, TN: Sumner County
    Public Library Board, 1979.

Dykeman, Wilma. _Tennessee: A History_.
    New York: Norton, 1984.

Fisk, Moses. Unpublished Papers.
    Tennessee State Library and
    Archives, Nashville.

Hays, Stockley Donelson. Letter.
    Jackson, _Papers_, II: 211.

"Jackson, Andrew." _Encyclopedia_
    Americana. 1986 ed.

Jackson, Andrew. _The Papers of Andrew_
    Jackson. Ed. Sam B. Smith and Harriet
    C. Owsley (Vol. 1); Harold D. Moser
    and Sharon MacPherson (Vol. 2). 4
    vols. Knoxville: U of Tennessee P,
    1980, 1984.

---. Misc. Papers. <u>The Messages and Papers of the Presidents</u>. Ed. James D. Richardson, 10 vols. Washington: n.p., 1900.

U. S. Congress. <u>American Archives</u>. Fourth series. Vol. 1. Washington: United States Congress, n.d.

Williams, Sampson, Letter. Jackson, <u>Papers</u>, II: 195.

Exercise 9.2 Write an alphabetical list of your sources in the spaces below. Submit it to your instructor for review, then use it to frame your final "Works Cited" page (see the previous page). Remember to indent five spaces for the second line and for any additional lines. Use an extra sheet if necessary.

_____

    _____

_____

    _____

_____

    _____

_____

    _____

    _____

_____

    _____

_____

Chapter 10—Formatting, Revising, Editing, and Proofreading

After completing the rough draft, you face three important tasks: you must 1) format and design the pages, 2) revise and edit, and 3) proofread.

• *Formatting* means to prepare the presentation of your paper according to page placement, spacing, and contents.

• *Revising* means to alter, amend, and improve the entire paper.

• *Editing* means preparing the draft for final writing by checking style, word choice, and grammar.

• *Proofreading* means examining the final manuscript to spot any last-minute errors.

10a Formatting

You may write your paper by hand, on a typewriter, or on a computer. In every case:

- Double-space all lines.

- Maintain a one-inch margin on each edge of the sheet.

- Indent paragraphs five spaces.

- Indent long quotations of four lines or more ten spaces.

- Indent poetry quotations of three lines or more ten spaces or center the lines of poetry evenly within your margins.

- Indent the second and succeeding lines of the bibliography entries five spaces.

- Center your title on the first page.

- Center the words "Works Cited" on the last page.

- Put your last name with the page number in the upper right corner of every page.

Note: Preserve all your notes and rough drafts. You may want to show how the paper grew from them.

Listing your name and course description

You do not need a separate title page; place the course information flush left at the top of your opening page.

List your full name, the teacher's name, and the date (see example, page 161). If you *do* write a separate title page, omit this course information from your opening page.

Writing a title page

Center the information on your title page, as shown below. Use an inverted pyramid order for the title (the longest line first) and follow with your name, your teacher's name, and the date. You may add the course title and name of the school if you like. However, do not underline the title, place it within quotation marks, or decorate the title with artwork. Here is a sample title page:

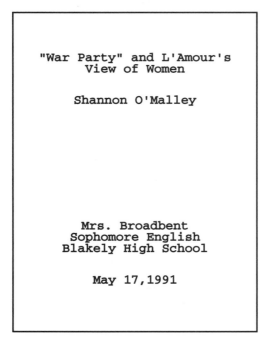

"War Party" and L'Amour's
View of Women

Shannon O'Malley

Mrs. Broadbent
Sophomore English
Blakely High School

May 17,1991

Submitting handwritten papers

A handwritten paper is shown next: it shows one writer's development of a research paper on Martin Luther King, Jr. The student's sources and notes are on the left-hand pages. The handwritten paper, submitted to her teacher, appears on the right-hand pages. Use it to guide the format and style of your paper.

In high school, Martin did so well that he skipped both the 9th and 12th grades. At the age of 15, he entered Morehouse College in Atlanta. King became an admirer of Benjamin E. Mays, Morehouse's president and a well-known scholar of black religion. Under Mays's influences, King decided to become a minister.
—from David J. Garrow, "King, Martin Luther, Jr." *World Book Encyclopedia*, 1990 ed.

WB 321

Being a bright child and teenager, King got to skip the 9th and 12th grades. When he was only 15, he got to enroll at Morehouse College. According to World Book he became a follower of Benjamin E. Mays. Mays was president of Morehouse College. He probably became a preacher because of this influence.

mar.tyr (**mahr** tir) n. 1. a person who suffers death rather than give up religious faith. 2. one who undergoes death or great suffering in support of a belief or cause or principle. **martyr** v. to put to death or torment as a martyr. **martyr.dom**.
—from *Oxford English Dictionary*, Avon paperback, 1980.

Most dictionaries define martyr as a person who suffers or dies in support of something or others, like a belief or a special reason. Rather than give in, the martyr would rather die.

Alisha L. Jerles

Mr. Ramsey

May 12, 1991

Martin Luther King, Jr.

Martin Luther King, Jr. was a black preacher who contributed a great deal to the Civil Rights Movement. Dr. King was born on January 15, 1929, in Atlanta, Georgia. Being a bright child and teenager, he skipped 9th and 12th grades. At the age of 15 he entered Morehouse College. According to one source, he became a follower of Benjamin E. Mays, who was president of Morehouse College (Garrow, "King" 321). He probably became a minister because of this influence.

As I think of Dr. King as a person, the word martyr comes to my mind. By definition, a martyr is a person who dies or suffers for a cause and would

Mohandas K. Gandhi, leader of the long struggle for independence, was shot to death in 1948. Gandhi had urged love for all people, including the untouchables. The assassin, a member of a high Hindu caste, hated Gandhi for his tolerance toward Moslems.
—from "India," *World Book Encyclopedia,* 1976 ed.

World Book vol. 10. page 106

Mohandas Gandhi in India was a great man who gave up his life for a cause of independence from Great Britain.

His most persuasive teacher, besides Jesus of Nazareth, proved to be Mohandas K. Gandhi, whose passive resistance movement had helped to free India from British domination. "From my Christian background I gained my ideals," King once said, "and from Gandhi my operational technique."

—from *Current Biography 1965,* page 221.

CB, page 221

Dr. King said, "From my Christian background I gained my ideals, and from Gandhi my operational technique" (CB 221).

rather die than give up or give in. Dr. King was a martyr. He knew he would probably get killed, but he marched and preached anyway.

Dr. King reminds me of President Abraham Lincoln. Both men carried on even though they were marked for death. Mohandas Gandhi in India is another person who gave up his life for a cause of independence from Great Britain ("India" 106). Dr. King said, "From my Christian background I gained my ideals, and from Gandhi my operational technique" (CB 221).

The Civil Rights Movement was his life's work. He traveled and marched and landed in jail time and again. He worked hard. "It was as if he were cramming a lifetime into each day" (Oates 456).

The victory by Dr. King at Montgomery, Alabama, when buses were desegregated,

In his acceptance speech in Oslo in December 1964 he spoke of the prize as an award to a movement, in recognition that "nonviolence is the answer to the crucial political and moral question of our time—the need for man to overcome oppression and violence without resorting to violence and oppression."
—from *Current Biography* 1965, page 222.

Nobel Speech
In his Nobel prize speech in 1965 he said that "nonviolence is the answer to the crucial political and moral question of our time -- the need for man to overcome oppression and violence without resorting to violence and oppression" (qtd. in CB 222).

He tried to joke about the danger he felt, about the possibility that he or one of his young aides might be gunned down. He would say, "If it's you, Andy, I sure will preach you a great eulogy," and then he would preach it to the amusement of everyone around. At other times, he would philosophize as always. "You know, I cannot worry about my safety; I cannot live in fear. I have to function. If there is any one fear I have conquered, it is the fear of death." And he would quote, "If a man has not found something worth giving his life for, he is not fit to live."
—from Stephen B. Oates, *Let the Trumpet Sound: The Life of Martin Luther King, Jr.* New York: Harper, 1982, page 455.

Oates 455
It seems that Dr. King, like a martyr, had made peace with death. He said: You know, I cannot worry about my safety; I cannot live in fear. I have to function. If there is any one fear I have conquered, it is the fear of death. (qtd. in Oates 455)

was important. C. Eric Lincoln says, "The Montgomery experience had taught black Americans the power of organization, the efficacy of sacrifice, and the dignity of suffering and nonviolence" (450). The word efficacy means to get the desired result.

In his Nobel prize speech in 1964 Dr. King said that "nonviolence is the answer to the crucial political and moral question of our time -- the need for man to overcome oppression and violence without resorting to violence and oppression" (qtd. in CB 222).

It seems that Dr. King had made peace with death. He said:

> You know, I cannot worry about my safety, I cannot live in fear. I have to function. If there is any one fear I have conquered, it is the fear of death. (qtd. in Oates 455)

Arrested on more than fifteen occasions, often assaulted, continually threatened, King symbolizes the courage, sacrifice, and suffering of the struggling Negro.
—from *Current Biography 1965*, page 220.

CB 1965, p. 220, says Dr. King was arrested more than fifteen times and probably was physically beaten on some occasions. He must have kept on trucking though cause he won the nobel prize and even went to Washington for the big speech -- I Have a Dream.

King knew nothing about any specific contracts against his life, but he realized that the Washington project made him more visible, increasing his chances of getting killed. He and many of his assistants had a feeling that he was being stalked now and that the end could come at any time: a knife thrust out of a crowd, a gunshot. . . . His staff worried constantly about his safety, but what could he do? he asked. He certainly couldn't go to the FBI or the police. And he was not going to carry a gun or let anyone around him do so either. That would violate everything he preached, everything he stood for. Anyway, what good would a gun do? Anybody who wanted to could shoot him at any time. Look how easily Oswald had killed Kennedy.
—From Stephen B. Oates, *Let the Trumpet Sound: The Life of Martin Luther King, Jr.* New York: Harper, 1982, page 455.

Oates 455

Dr. King was preoccupied with death. Stephen Oates says Dr. King felt "he was being stalked now and that the end would come at any time; a knife thrust out of a crowd, a gunshot..." (455). But he would not carry a gun for protection. Oates says that Dr. King did not want to violate his own rules of nonviolence (455).

He was committed to his cause. One source explained that Dr. King was arrested more than fifteen times and physically beaten on some occasions (CB 220). But he fought the fight, going to Washington with his "I Have a Dream" speech. And before his death he had started a poor people's campaign which angered many people and caused more threats on his life.

Stephen Oates explains that Dr. King "was being stalked now and that the end would come at any time; a knife thrust out of a crowd, a gunshot..." (455). But Dr. King would not carry a gun for protection. Oates says that Dr. King did not want to violate his own rules of nonviolence (455).

The night before he died, Dr. King said:

> I just want to do God's will. And He's allowed me to go up to the mountain, and I've looked over,

Well, I don't know what will happen now. We've got some difficult days ahead. But it really doesn't matter with me now, because I have been to the mountaintop. And I don't mind. Like anybody, I would like to live a long life. Longevity has its place. But I'm not concerned about that now. I just want to do God's will. And he's allowed me to go up to the mountain, and I've looked over, and I've seen the promised land. I may not get there with you. But I want you to know tonight, that we, as a people will get to the promised land. And so I'm happy tonight. I'm not worried about anything. I'm not fearing any man. Mine eyes have seen the glory of the coming of the Lord.
—from David J. Garrow, *Bearing the Cross: Martin Luther King, Jr., and the Southern Christian Leadership Conference,* New York: Morrow, 1986, page 621.

King speech in Garrow 621
I just wanted to do God's will. And He's allowed me to go up to the mountain, and I've looked over, and I've seen the promised land. I may not get there with you. But I want you to know tonight, that we, as a people, will get to the promised land. And so I'm happy tonight. I'm not worried about anything. I'm not fearing any man. Mine eyes have seen the glory of the coming of the Lord.

and I've seen the promised land.
I may not get there with you. But
I want you to know tonight, that we,
as a people, will get to the promised land.
And so I'm happy tonight. I'm not
worried about anything. I'm not
fearing any man. Mine eyes have
seen the glory of the coming of
the Lord. (Garrow, Bearing 621)

On the next day Dr. King was gunned down in
memphis. He died as a martyr. But he probably
would reject any suggestion that we call him a
saint or anything of that sort. Dr. King's sister
said, "He wasn't saintly at all" (Christain King Farris,
qtd. in Turner 32). We cannot automatically call a
martyr a saint. He had failings just like everybody,
so he would probably ask us to honor him by
living a life of peace and nonviolence.

Garrow, David J. <u>Bearing the Cross.</u> New York: Morrow, 1986.

> Garrow, David J.
>   <u>Bearing the Cross</u>.
>   New York: Morrow, 1986.

Oates, Stephen B. <u>Let the Trumpet Sound: The Life of Martin Luther King, Jr.</u>
   New York: Harper, 1982.

> Oates, Stephen B.
>   <u>Let the Trumpet Sound: The</u>
>   <u>Life of Martin Luther King, Jr.</u>
>   New York: Harper, 1982.

Turner, Renee D. "The Private Side of a Public Man: Martin Luther King, Jr."
   <u>Ebony</u> Jan. 1991: 32+.

> Turner, Renée D.
>   "The Private Side of a Public
>   Man: Martin Luther King, Jr."
>   <u>Ebony</u> Jan. 1991: 32+.

Works Cited

Garrow, David J. Bearing the Cross.
New York: Morrow, 1986.

---. "King, Martin Luther, Jr." World
Book Encyclopedia. 1990 ed.

"India." World Book Encyclopedia. 1976 ed.

"King, Martin Luther, Jr." Current Biography
Yearbook 1965. New York: Wilson, 1965.

Lincoln, C. Eric. "King, Martin Luther, Jr."
Encyclopedia Americana. 1990 ed.

Oates, Stephen B. Let the Trumpet Sound:
The Life of Martin Luther King, Jr.
New York: Harper, 1982.

Turner, Renée D. "The Private Side of a
Public Man: Martin Luther King, Jr."
Ebony Jan. 1991: 32+.

Typing your paper

If you type your paper, you should also follow the rules cited above for margins, spacing, and indentations. Use white bond paper and type on only one side of the sheet. Use a fresh ribbon. Do not decorate the paper with handdrawn artwork or reproductions unless the paper's subject demands it. Do not use erasable paper which smears your typing and sometimes obliterates the wording. And always proofread carefully.

Writing your paper on a computer

If you know the technology, by all means use a computer to generate a polished paper. You can store and retrieve your notes and drafts, revise by moving blocks of material from one place to another, and edit quickly on a monitor screen. After keyboarding the paper one time, you can get multiple printouts as you revise and proofread.

With some computers, you can create graphic designs, you can show italic typeface rather than underlining, and you can even print with various type fonts.

Take advantage of the computer's special features to edit the paper. If software is available to check your spelling, your grammar, and your style, use it. See the appendix, pages 208–216, for details about using word processing.

10b Revising

If you are advised to make "global" revisions, you must be willing to rewrite and/or rearrange your entire paper.

Begin by examining your *introduction* for: a thesis, a clear direction or plan of development, and a sense of your involvement with the reader. See pages 111–119 for additional tips and guidelines about the opening section for research papers.

Examine your *body* for: a clear sequence of major statements, appropriate and effective evidence to support your key ideas, and transitions that move the reader effectively from one block of material to another. See pages 120–132 for additional guidelines.

Examine your *ending* for: a conclusion that is drawn from the evidence, one that evolves logically from the introduction and the body, and one that clearly conveys your position and interpretation. See pages 133–140 for additional information about writing the conclusion.

Work your way through your entire paper again and again. Keep in mind that even the best of writers often prepare multiple drafts.

10c Editing

Read through your paper to study your sentence structure and word choices. Cut phrases and sentences that do not advance your main ideas or that merely repeat what your sources have already stated. Look for ways to change "to be" verbs (is, are, was) to stronger, active verbs. Try to convert passive structures to active ones. Confirm that your paraphrases and quotations flow smoothly within your text. Check your spelling. Note the editing by one student in the following example:

```
One critic calls television "junk food"

                      television does
(Fransecky 717). ~~and I think too much~~ᵉ
            watching∧takeş time from other things,

        it also
but∧ ~~television doose~~ give∧ us a few    ˢ

cultural programs ~~and some good novels~~ᵉ

~~that we can tape,~~ but it should do

                 children's
more to encourage ~~their~~ reading and

writing.
```

Carefully review the form and punctuation you have used. The following paper, with explanatory notes, can serve as a model for you.

Give name and page in upper right corner.

Shannon O'Malley

Mrs. Broadbent

May 17, 1991

Give name, teacher, and date flush left.

"War Party" and Louis L'Amour's View of Women

Center the title

Louis L'Amour is a famous writer of western stories, such as *Hondo*, *The Daybreakers*, and *The Lonesome Gods*. According to one source, more than one hundred thirty million copies of his books have been sold (Farrell et al. 429). His story "War Party" is told by Bud Miles. Bud describes the western frontier in this way:

Use Italics if your computer supports them

> The world seemed to bust wide open, and suddenly the horizons spread out and a man wasn't cramped anymore. The pinched-up villages and the narrowness of towns, all that was gone. The horizons simply exploded and rolled back into enormous distance, with nothing around but prairie and sky. (L'Amour 418-19)

"Farrell et al." means "Farrell and others"; all names appear in the bibliography entry.

Indent long quotations 10 spaces.

People had to grow up fast on the frontier. Bud is a 12-year-old boy who must become a man overnight because his dad gets killed by Indians. Both Bud and his mother demonstrate courage, though, by facing up to the Indians and the hatred of their fellow travelers.

Do not enclose a long quotation within quotations marks. The in-text citation goes outside the period after a long, indented quotation.

For some people the frontier of the American west was an opportunity, for some it was a challenge, and for others it was a dangerous territory that was best avoided. To Bud in "War Party" the frontier was adventure. To his mother it would be "home." Bud thought home was something they had left. His mother explained, "Home is where we're going now, and we'll know it when we find it" (420). Bud heard her definition, but he also said:

> She might tell us that home was where we're going, but I knew home was where ma was, a warm and friendly place with biscuits on the table and fresh-made butter. We wouldn't have a real home until ma was there and we had a fire going. Only I'd build the fire. (420)

Bud is eager to grow up. His mother must accept more responsibility because of the death of Mr. Miles, who was killed by Indians early on the journey. Together the mother and her son make a good team. They go where "the horizons simply exploded and rolled back into enormous distance, with nothing around but prairie and sky" (419). Life will not be easy. They will face many hardships but stick together.

The story shows us three stages for the frontier hero or heroine. The first step is to cross the Mississippi River. The second stage is to continue the journey despite death, danger,

Introduce long quotations with a colon.

Blend short quotations into your text, omitting a capital letter if the phrase flows naturally into your sentence.

poor weather, and lack of food. The third stage (the most dangerous for Mr. Miles) is to face the envy and jealousy of fellow travelers. Bud and his mother survive all three tests.

Bud is still a child, but he is tough and smart. He kills a buffalo, and later on he kills an antelope on the run. He knows when to remain silent and when to speak out boldly. But sometimes a child is only as strong as adults will allow. In "War Party" Bud rises to a new level because his mother lets it happen. She tells Buchanan, "I have my man. Bud is almost thirteen and accepts responsibility. I could ask for no better man" (420). At the end of the story Bud shows his courage by standing up to Mr. Buchanan. He says: "Mr. Buchanan, I may be little and may be a fool, but this here rifle doesn't care who pulls its trigger" (427).

Bud's mother is the true heroine. She is the one who decides to continue west after Bud's father has been killed. In fact, she killed the Indian who shot the arrow at her husband. She faces up to Mr. Buchanan, who wanted her to turn back, and she faces up to the Sioux chief. She makes a home in the west despite the problems.

The Indians were only one problem. The prejudice of the pioneers was another. One of the rules of the wagon was: "There has to be a man with every wagon" (420). A few travelers condemned Mrs. Miles. Later, when she faced up to the Sioux chief, many people again thought she was out of place. The pioneers thought that confronting an Indian was a man's job.

Place page citations in the text within parentheses after the quotation mark and before the period. Compare this use with that of long quotations.

She spoke the Sioux language and was able to calm the chief and his braves. She really is the one who saved the wagon train. But the people were suspicious of her. How did she know the Sioux language? Some pioneers wanted to kick her off the wagon train because she was surely an Indian. But, in fact, she was not an Indian at all. She grew up playing with the Sioux in Minnesota and drew upon that knowledge to save her family.

Louis L'Amour's characters were drawn from the actual people who lived the frontier life. One old man had been a captive of the Apaches for many childhood years (*CB* 203). L'Amour used the old man as a model for a character: "He was a man who knew all about the Apaches, how they lived, how they worked, how they fought" (qtd. in *CB* 203). L'Amour adds, "In much of his thinking, he was still an Apache."

L'Amour is well known as a writer about the west. Readers may think of him as a male chauvinist like Mr. Buchanan. But L'Amour likes women. He shows how tough they can be. Mrs. Miles holds her own in a male world. L'Amour says:

> There's an old saying in the West:
> The cowards didn't start and the weak
> didn't make it. That was as true for
> the women as it was for the men. Many
> times a woman lost her husband in the
> move West, and she took on the work

Do not hyphenate any words at the end of the lines, even if it causes an unusually short line.

Abbreviate within the in-text citations but not in the text (*CB* stands for *Current Biography*)

herself and filed the land claim
herself. No, I'm not the least bit
sexist—very much to the contrary.
I'm a great admirer of women. (Qtd.
in *CA* 25:266)

 L'Amour also says, "My whole feeling about
the American West, the American frontier, is
that a lot more was happening than just a bunch
of gunfights or Indian battles" (qtd. in *CB*
205). "War Party" shows that people were making
homes, like the one described by Bud:

> A long valley lay across our route,
> with mountains beyond it, and tall
> grass wet with rain, and a flat
> bench on the mountainside seen
> through a gray veil of a light
> shower falling. There was that bench,
> with the white trunks of aspen on the
> mountainside beyond it looking like
> the ranks of slim soldiers guarding
> the bench against the storms.
>
> > "Ma," I said.
> > "All right, Bud," she said
> > quietly, "We've come home."
> > (427)

The reader will know to look for L'Amour's speech in *Current Biography*, not in a book by L'Amour.

Do not write "The End" on your last page or add any sort of art work.

Begin the "Works Cited" on an entirely new page.

Works Cited

Farrell, Edmund J., Ouida H. Clapp, and Karen J. Kuehner. *Patterns in Literature.*Glenview:Scott, 1991.

Note the cross reference to the Farrell anthology.

L'Amour, Louis. "War Party." Farrell et al. 418-27.

"Louis L'Amour." *Contemporary Authors.* Ed. Hal May and Deborah A Straub. Detroit: Gale, n.d. 25: 261-67.

L'Amour is the author of one work and his name is the title of three other works.

"Louis L'Amour." *Current Biography Yearbook 1980.* New York: Wilson, 1981. 203-208.

"Louis L'Amour." *World Book Encyclopedia.* 1990 ed.

Editing to avoid discriminatory language

Do not stereotype any person, regardless of gender, race, nationality, creed, age, or handicap. Your writing should be precise. Follow these guidelines to avoid discriminatory language:

1. Review the accuracy of your statements.

Discriminatory:

```
Old people walk with difficulty.
```

• How old is old?

• Do *all* old people walk with difficulty?

• Are the elderly the only persons who walk with difficulty?

Nondiscriminatory:

```
Mr. Brown walks with difficulty.
```

2. Use plural subjects so that nonspecific, plural pronouns are grammatically correct: "The technicians keep their equipment in sterile condition." Do be careful, though, because the plural is easily overused and often inappropriate. For example, some people now use a plural pronoun with the singular *everybody, everyone, anybody, anyone, each one* in order to avoid a masculine reference.

Sexist:

Each author of the Pre-Raphaelite period
produced <u>his</u> best work prior to 1865.

Colloquial:

Each author of the Pre-Raphaelite period
produced <u>their</u> best work prior to 1865.

Formal:

Authors of the Pre-Raphaelite period produced
their best works prior to 1865.

3. Change the wording of the sentence so that a pronoun is unnecessary. Note these correct sentences:

The doctor prepared the necessary surgical
equipment without interference.

Each technician must maintain laboratory
equipment in sterile condition.

4. Use pronouns denoting gender only when necessary to specify gender or when gender has been previously established. The use of a specifier (*the, this, that*) is often helpful. In directions and informal settings, the pronoun "you" is appropriate. Note these correct sentences:

```
Mary, as a new laboratory technician, must learn
to maintain her equipment in sterile condition.

The lab technician maintains this equipment in
sterile condition.

Each of you should maintain your equipment in
sterile condition.
```

5. In general, avoid formal titles (Dr., Gen., Mrs., Ms., Lt., Professor, and so forth). Avoid their equivalents in other languages (Mme, Dame, Monsieur). First mention of a person requires the full name (for example, Ernest Hemingway or Margaret Mead) and thereafter requires only usage of the surname (Hemingway or Mead). Use Emily Brontë and thereafter use Brontë, *not* Miss Brontë.

10d Proofreading

After the final copy is finished, whether handwritten or typed, proofread it carefully. Typing the paper, or having it typed by somebody else, does not relieve you of the responsibility of proofreading; if anything, it requires you to be doubly careful. Marring a page with a few handwritten corrections is better than leaving errors in your text.

Specifically, check for errors in sentence structure, spelling, and punctuation. Avoid dividing a word at the end of a line. Read each quotation for accuracy in wording and documentation. Double-check citations to be certain that each one is listed on your "Works Cited" page at the end of the paper.

Chapter 11—APA Style

You may sometime be asked to write a paper in APA style, which is governed by *The Publication Manual of the American Psychological Association.* This style has gained wide acceptance in academic circles. APA style is used in the social sciences, and versions similar to it are used in the biological sciences, business, and the earth sciences.

You need to understand two basic ideas that govern this style. First, a scientific paper attempts to show what has been proven true by research in a narrowly defined area, so it requires the past tense when you refer to procedures completed in the past. ("Johnson stipulated" or "the work of Elmford and Mills showed"). Second, the scientific community considers the year of publication as vital information, so they feature it immediately after any named source, like this: (Johnson & Marshall, 1991). These two primary distinctions, and others, are explained below.

11a Proper tense for an APA paper

Verb tense is an indicator that distinguishes papers in the humanities from those in the natural and social sciences. MLA style, as shown in previous chapters, requires you to use present tense when you refer to a cited work ("Johnson *stipulates*" or "the work of Elmford and Mills *shows*"). In contrast, APA style requires you to use past tense or present perfect tense ("Marshall stipulated" or "the work of Elmford and Mills has demonstrated"). APA style does require present tense when you discuss the results, usually in your conclusion (for example, *the results confirm* or *the study indicates*).

A paper in the humanities (MLA style) makes universal assertions, so it uses the historical present tense:

```
"It was the best of times, it was the worst of
times," writes Charles Dickens about the
eighteenth century.
```

```
Johnson argues that sociologist Norman Manway
has a "narrow-minded view of clerics and their
role in nineteenth century fiction" (64).
```

In contrast, a paper in APA style attempts to place limits on its claims and wishes to prove only one point. It therefore stipulates use of the past tense or the present perfect tense with its citations:

```
Matthews (1989) designed the experiment, and
since that time several investigators have used
the method (Thurman, 1990; Jones, 1991).
```

Note the differences in the verbs of these next two passages whenever the verbs refer to a cited work.

MLA style:

```
Television encourages reading, which in turn
improves language competence. Beyond the one-
time motivation of children who responded to
Fonzie's request for a library card, research
indicates that good programming improves reading
and can increase library lendings. The
Himmelweit study in Great Britain, Television
and the Child, confirms that "television in the
long run encourages children to read books, a
```

conclusion that can be reinforced by evidence
from libraries, books clubs, and publishing
companies" (Postman 33). Dr. Himmelweit *makes*
this point: "Book reading comes into its own,
not despite television but because of it" (qtd.
in Postman 33).

APA style:

Television encourages reading, which in turn
improves language competence. Beyond the one-
time motivation of children who responded to
Fonzie's request for a library card, research
has indicated that good programming *improved*
reading and *increased* library lendings. The
Himmelweit study in Great Britain, *Television
and the Child, confirmed* that "television in the
long run encourages children to read books, a
conclusion that can be reinforced by evidence
from libraries, books clubs, and publishing
companies" (Postman, 1961, p. 33). Dr.
Himmelweit *made* this point: "Book reading comes
into its own, not despite television but because
of it" (cited in Postman, 1961, p. 33).

As shown first, MLA style requires that you use the
present tense both for personal comments and for
introducing the sources. In MLA style the ideas and the
words of the authorities, theoretically, remain in print
and continue to be true in the universal present. APA
style, second, requires that you use present tense for
your own comments but requires the past tense for

sources cited. The sources *have tested* a hypothesis or the sources *reported* the results of the test.

present tense is correct here

past tense is correct here

```
The danger of steroid use exists for every age
group, even youngsters. Lloyd and Mercer (1991)
reported on six incidents of liver damage to 14-
year-old swimmers who used steriods.
```

11b Using in-text citations in APA style

APA style requires an in-text citation to the name of the author and the year of publication.

```
Conniff (1990) showed that one federal agency,
the Bureau of Land Management, failed to protect
the natural treasures of public land holdings,
and Struble (1991) offered evidence that BLM
serves the needs of ranchers, not the public.
```

Provide a page number only when you quote the exact words of a source, and *do* use "p." or "pp." with page numbers.

```
Conniff (1990, p. 33) explained that the bureau
must "figure out how to keep the land healthy
while also accommodating cowpokes, strip miners,
dirt bikers, birdwatchers, and tree huggers,
all vocal, all willing to sue for their
conflicting rights."
```

If you do not use the author's name in your text, place the name within the parenthetical citation.

```
It has been shown that the Bureau of Land
Management often sacrifices wildlife and the
environment to benefit miners and ranchers
(Conniff, 1990; Struble, 1991).
```

When a work has two or more authors, use "&" in citations only, not in the text.

Use "&" for citations

```
It has been reported (Werner & Throckmorton,
1990) that toxic levels exceeded the maximum
allowed levels each year since 1983.
```

Use "and" in the text

```
Werner and Throckmorton (1990, pp. 457-464)
offered statistics on their analysis of water
samples from six rivers and announced without
reservation that "the waters are unfit for human
consumption, pose dangers to swimmers,  and
produce contaminated fish that may cause
salmonella."
```

Sometimes you must make an in-text citation to a textbook, casebook, or anthology. If so, refer to the source in normal APA style (see pages 195–197).

```
One writer stressed that two out of every three new
jobs in the 1990s will go to women (Bailey, 1988).
```

Exercise 11.1 In the second (b) version of each sentence below make two corrections. Change the verb tense in references to a cited author and change the in-text citations from MLA style to APA style by filling the blank spaces of the parentheses. (Note: Assume that the year of publication is 1990.)

1a MLA style. Shirley Taggert defends the role of women reporters in men's locker rooms after sporting events, saying "reporters should not be judged by gender or denied access to athletes for interviews" (34).
1b APA style. Taggert (   ) defend_____ the role of women reporters in men's locker rooms after sporting events, saying "reporters should not be judged by their gender or denied access to athletes for interviews following any athletic contest" (   ).

2a MLA style. One critic reports that Vietnam and Desert Storm had a destabilizing effect on our national psyche (Harden 284).
2b APA style. One critic (   ) report_____ that Vietnam and Desert Storm had a destabilizing effect on our national psyche.

3a MLA style. "Young people cannot be expected to go to college for the general good of mankind" (Caroline Bird 352).
3b APA style. One source (   ) has assert_____ that "young people cannot be expected to go to college for the general good of mankind."

Exercise 11.2 Label *C (correct)* the sentences below that properly cite the following source in APA style.

The distinction between active and passive euthanasia is thought to be crucial for medical ethics. The idea is that it is permissible, at least in some cases, to withhold treatment and allow a patient to die, but it is never permissible to take any direct action designed to kill the patient.
—James Rachels, 1975, p. 78

_____ **1.** One source labels passive euthanasia as withholding treatment.

_____ **2.** One source (Rachels, 1975) has labeled passive euthanasia as withholding treatment.

_____ **3.** Rachels (1975) has distinguished passive euthanasia, "to withhold treatment," and active euthanasia, "to take any direct action designed to kill the patient" (p. 78).

_____ **4.** Medical ethics has determined that it is never permissible to take any direct action designed to kill the patient (Rachels, 1975).

_____ **5.** The differences between passive and active euthanasia has been determined (Rachels, 1975).

11c Preparing the bibliography page

Use the title "References" for your bibliography page. Alphabetize the entries and double-space throughout. Type the first line of each entry flush left, and indent succeeding lines three (3) spaces.

Book (APA style)

```
Carter J. (1988). An outdoor journal: Adventures
    and reflections. New York: Bantam.
```

List the author (surname first with initials for given names), year of publication within parentheses, title of the book underlined and with only first word of the title and any subtitle capitalized (but capitalize proper nouns), place of publication, and publisher. In the publishers, name omit the words *Publishing, Company,* or *Inc.,* but otherwise give a full name: Harcourt Brace Jovanovich, Florida State University Press, HarperCollins.

Magazine (APA style)

```
Conniff, R. (1990, September). Once the secret
    domain of miners and ranchers, the BLM is
    going public. Smithsonian, pp. 30-47.
```

List author, the date of publication (year, month, and the specific day for weekly and bi-monthly magazines), title of the article without quotation marks and with only the first word capitalized, name of the magazine underlined with all major words capitalized, and inclusive page numbers preceded by "p." or "pp."

Journal (APA style)

Mielke, K. W. (1988). Television in the social
    studies classroom. <u>Social Education</u>, <u>52</u>, 362–365.

List author, year, title of the article without quotation marks and with only the first word capitalized, name of the journal underlined and with all major words capitalized, volume number underlined, inclusive page numbers not preceded by "p." or "pp."

Newspaper (APA style)

Raymond, C. (1990, September 12). Global
    migration will have widespread impact on
    society, scholars say. <u>Chronicle of
    Higher Education</u>, pp. A1, A6.

List author, date (year, month, and day), title of article with only first word and proper nouns capitalized, name of newspaper in capitals and underlined, and the section with all discontinuous page numbers.

Encyclopedia (APA style)

"Acne." (1990). <u>World book encyclopedia</u>.
   Chicago: World Book.

List author (if available), title of the article, year of the edition used, title of the encyclopedia, place, and publisher.

Part of a book (APA style)

Hartley, J. T., Harker, J. O., & Walsh, D. A.
   (1980). Contemporary issues and new
   directions in adult development of learning
   and memory. In L. W. Poon (Ed.), <u>*Aging in*</u>
   <u>*the 1980s: Psychological issues*</u> (pp. 239-
   252). Washington, DC: American Psychological
   Association.

List author(s), date, chapter or section title, editor (with name in normal order) preceded by "In" and followed by "(Ed.)" or "(Eds.)," the name of the book, page numbers to the specific section of the book cited, place of publication, and publisher.

Textbook, casebook, anthology (APA style)

Make a primary reference to the anthology:

Vesterman, W. (Ed.) (1991). <u>Readings for</u>
   <u>the 21st century</u>. Boston: Allyn & Bacon.

Thereafter, make cross references to the primary source, in this case Vesterman. Note: these entries should be mingled with all others on the reference page in alphabetical order so that a cross reference may appear before or after the primary source. The year cited should be the date when the cited work was published, not when the Vesterman book was published; such information is usually found in a headnote, footnote, or list of credits at the front or back of the anthology.

Bailey, J. (1988). Jobs for women in the
    nineties. In Vesterman, pp. 55-63.

Fallows, D. (1982). Why mothers should
    stay home. In Vesterman, pp. 69-77.

Steinem, G. (1972). Sisterhood. In
    Vesterman, pp. 48-53.

Vesterman, W. (Ed.) (1991). <u>Readings for
    the 21st century</u>. Boston: Allyn & Bacon.

The alternative to the style shown above is to provide a complete entry for every one of the authors cited from the casebook (in which case you do not need a separate entry to Vesterman):

Bailey, J. (1988). Jobs for women in the
    nineties. In W. Vesterman (Ed.), (1991),
    <u>*Readings for the 21st century*</u> (pp. 55-63).
    Boston: Allyn & Bacon.

Fallows, D. (1982). Why mothers should
    stay home. In W. Vesterman (Ed.),
    (1991), Readings for the 21st century (pp.
    69-77). Boston: Allyn & Bacon.

Steinem, G. (1972). Sisterhood. In W.
    Vesterman (Ed.), (1991), *Readings for the
    21st century* (pp. 48-53). Boston: Allyn &
    Bacon.

Abstract (APA style, cited from an abstract only)

Published abstract:

Misumi, J., & Fujita, M. (1982). Effects of PM
    organizational development in supermarket
    organization. *Japanese Journal of
    Experimental Social Psychology, 21*, 93-111.
    (From Psychological Abstracts, 1982, 68,
    Abstract No. 11474).

Unpublished abstract:

Havens, N. B. (1982). Verbalized symbolic play
    of pre-school children in two types of play
    environments. Abstract of doctoral
    dissertation, Temple University. (From
    Dissertation Abstracts International, 1982,
    42, 5058A.

Book with corporate author, third edition (APA style)

American Psychiatric Association. (1980).
   Diagnostic statistical manual of mental
   disorders (3rd ed.). Washington, DC: Author.

Report (APA style)

Lance, J. C. (1990). Housing regulations (KU No.
   90-16). Lawrence, KS: Media Center.

Review (APA style)

Jones, S. L. (1991, January 6). The power of
   motivation [Review of Body heat].
   Contemporary Film Review, p. 18.

Nonprint material (APA style)

Corborn, W. H. (1990, November 3). [On facing
   the fears caused by nightmares] Interview.
   Lexington, KY.

Purple, W. C. (Producer). (1990). Hitting the
   backhand [Videotape]. Nashville: Sports
   Network.

```
Landers, J., Woolfe, R. T., & Balcher, C.
    (1990). Geometry games: Level two [Computer
    program]. Emporia, KS: Mediaworks.
```

Exercise 11.3 Write the following bibliography references in APA style.

Book: John Newson and Elizabeth Newson, <u>Toys and Playthings in Development and Remediation</u>. New York, Pantheon Books, 1979.

Magazine: Gary Legwold, "Fitness Matters: Good News About Shaping Up," <u>Better Homes and Gardens</u>, November 1990, page 54.

Journal: M. J. Mendelson, H. M. Haith, and P. S. Goldman-Rakic. "Facing Scanning and Responsiveness to Social Cues." <u>Developmental Psychology</u>, 1982, Vol. 18, pages 222–228.

_____

Newspaper: Tim Friend, "Lyme Disease Vaccine Gets First Test," <u>USA Today</u>, Oct. 26, 1990, page 1A.

_____

Part of a book: "Mental Health," by Emily Ford, chapter 6 of <u>Health, Behavior, and the Environment</u>, edited by Daniel Farnsworth, 1990, New York, McMann Publishers.

_____

Advertising in the Classroom

Lawrence Thompson

Northeast High School

Running Head: Advertising

Advertising in the Classroom

Young people spend money just like adults. They do not spend as much as adults, but they are a powerful force in the nation's economy. Big companies spend millions of dollars in advertising to reach kids, and they always look for new ways to do it. Now advertisers have entered the school classroom. Channel One sends a daily news broadcast into the schools but it comes with a set of commercials. Teachers distribute free educational materials with the logos of McDonald's, Nutrasweet, Chef Boyardee, and others. Student clubs have to sell candy and other things to raise funds. One advertising executive admitted:

> It isn't enough to just advertise on television. You've got to reach kids throughout the day—in school, as they're shopping in the mall . . . or at the movies. You've got to become part of the fabric of their lives. (Herman, 1990, cited in "Selling," p. 518)

Advertisers have bought their way into the classroom with the free educational materials, but their target is the dollar bill of the student, not the mind of the student.

Grade-school children and young people at high school feel pressured to buy certain products. Students now must wear the correct brand-name clothing, which in one school might be 501 jeans and Nike sneakers and elsewhere it might be Duckheads and Bass Weejuns. Clothing makes for social status. Students feel the pressure in all areas—choice of food, knowledge of the movies, ability to get a six-pack of beer for the gang. One source reported, "Children learn and want to be consumers at an ever earlier age" (Willis, 1987, p. 406).

The methods sometimes force a kid to purchase a product. For example, one concerned group, Action for Children's Television (ACT), wanted to forbid interactive weapons like Captain Power on television because the program required children or their parents to buy a toy in order to participate fully. Such games have established the "haves and the have-nots" (Kantrowitz, 1987, p. 72).

Critics have focused on other methods that advertisers use (Moore & Linnon, 1989, pp.36-39; "Selling," pp. 518-21). Here is a brief list:

1. Ads disguised as educational material
2. Children's clubs that circulate advertising
3. Scoreboards and vending machines with logos
4. Fund-raisers that sell brand-name goods
5. Wall displays with the logos of sponsors
6. Brand-name equipment supplied free or at a deep discount
7. Channel One's news with commercials

8. Newspapers, yearbooks, and even a
video yearbook (all with advertising)

This writer does not deny the value of some
free materials. Many of the educational
pamphlets, filmstrips, and videos serve a
valuable purpose. Our school newspaper and
yearbook would cease to exist without
advertising dollars. Nevertheless, a commercial
in the school does prompt the student to buy
that product, and companies do work on the minds
of students. Noore and Linnon (1989) have warned:

> Educators, school authorities and
> parents, preoccupied with issues like
> drugs and poor test scores, are only
> dimly aware of how successful and
> sophisticated companies have become in
> promoting products to and through schools.
> (p. 34)

Most advertising is not even subtle. It is
direct selling by Bic, McDonald's, Pizza Hut,
and other companies. One school superintendent
reported, "The problem is, they want us to sell
access to our kids' minds, and we have no right,
morally or ethically, to do that" (Bill Honig,
cited in Noore & Linnon, 1989, p. 40). Rudinow
(1990) has reported the results of Channel One's
intrusion in this manner:

> On the face of it, this looks like
> another triumph of the American
> entrepreneurial spirit. The schools get
> high technology, the teachers get lesson
> plans, the students get information in an

entertaining format, the districts get results, Whittle [owner of Channel One] gets a cash cow, and the sponsors get a captive audience. (p. 70)

Questions come to mind. If Channel One is such a valuable teaching tool, why is it a profit-making venture? Why didn't our teachers come up with the idea first? Why didn't the government support the plan? Rudinow (1990, p. 71) has coined the word "advercation" to describe advertising disguised as education. He said that advertisers want a "passive, unreflective" audience as opposed to the efforts of teachers to develop the "inquisitive, creative, skeptical, reflective, self-reliant habits of mind" of their students (p. 72). Channel One's editor responded in this way:

We believe we have created an especially powerful tool to help teachers remedy the woeful ignorance of American teenagers about current events, geography, and related subjects. (Rukeyser, 1990, p. 75)

Peggy Charren, president of Action for Children's Television, answered Rukeyser: "The whole thing is still being paid for by selling kids to advertisers" (cited in Zuckerman, 1989, p. 56). With this paper I do not mean to condemn technology in the classroom. Good things are happening. Castleberry (1989) has described the use of technology for "distance learning" by which students in remote areas can learn by using a "satellite television network" and an "electronic chalkboard" (p. 37). Programs like

KIDSNET have value. KIDSNET is a data base that has thousands of programs for students. Teachers can also use over 20,000 radio and television programs on special needs by subject, curriculum, and grade level (see Mielke, 1988).

Channel One and printed brochures with company logos can serve classroom needs, but they should be accompanied by lessons from a skillful teacher. Rudinow (1990, p. 72) warned: "What advertisers want is a passive, unreflective, credulous audience, susceptible to the dictates of external authority." What students need are teachers who encourage us to be independent.

Maybe this issue of commercialism in the classroom is not very important. Most students seem to enjoy the educational packages like Channel One and McDonald's school magazine. But many students are overweight because of poor diets. Some get violent because of what they see on television. Others smoke deadly cigarettes, and too many drink alcohol. Can we blame advertising and the companies behind the products? Yes, I think so, and the Consumer's Union has agreed, saying, "We believe promotions that target children should be held to higher standards than those aimed at adults" ("Selling," p. 521). Teachers ought to screen these advertising "gifts" that appear in the classroom, and students need to get smart and not be fooled by advertising. If a product is good, we'll find it.

References

Castleberry, J. (1989). Satellite learning—a
vision for the future. NASSP Bulletin, 73, 35-41.

Erickson, E. H. (1977). Toys and reasons: Stages
in the ritualization of experience. New
York: W. W. Norton.

Rantrowitz, B. (1987, November 2). High-tech
toys. Newsweek, pp. 71-72.

Mielke, K. (1988). Television in the social
studies classroom. Social Education, 52, 362-365.

Moore, T., & Linnon, N. (1989, November 6). The
selling of our schools. U.S. News & World
Report, pp. 34-40.

Rudinow, J. (1989, December-January). Channel
One whittles away at education. Educational
Leadership, pp. 70-73.

Rukeyser, W. S. (1989, December-January). No
hidden agenda: A response to Rudinow.
Educational Leadership, pp. 74-75.

Selling to children. (1990, August). Consumer
Reports, pp. 518-521.

Willis, S. (1987). Gender as commodity. South
Atlantic Quarterly, 86, 403-21.

Zuckerman, L. (1989, June 19). Teacher or trojan
horse? Time, p. 56.

Appendix: Writing with Word Processing

Many students now use computers for writing their research papers. This new technology has several advantages. It saves time because you type the text just once. After that, you need only enter your corrections; you don't need to retype your whole paper. The computer enables you to store and retrieve notes and to maintain your list of sources. You can print your notes and edit them on the printed copy as well as on the computer monitor. You may even be able to use special software to review your writing style and your spelling.

Storing and retrieving notes, documents, and bibliography sources

The computer affects note-taking strategies in several ways:

1) Record the bibliography information for each source in a file named BIBLIO (*bibliography*) or WC *(works cited)*. This file, kept in alphabetical order, will provide the final "Works Cited" page. Chapters 9 and 11 show the correct form of various entries.

2) Write your notes into the word processor using one of two methods.

> **a.** Write all notes into a single file, labeled with a short title, such as NOTES. Your notes can then be moved around easily within the one document by BLOCK moves which will transfer them quickly into your TEXT document.

> **b.** Write each note as a separate temporary file so that each can be moved later into the appropriate section of your TEXT file by a COPY or READ command. You can easily move blocks of material when you revise the paper.

3) Try to write your computer notes in a complete, fluid writing style just as you would if you were working with paper and pen. You can transfer the notes into your rough draft and make minor revisions to fit the context.

4) When you begin writing, copy notes directly into your rough draft by moving blocks or by transferring files. However, keep original notes on file in case you need them again.

Entering your text into a computer

A word processing system on any computer functions much like a typewriter, with several advantages. Just be sure to SAVE your material often, perhaps as you complete each page. This command inscribes your writing onto the disk or tape. If the computer suddenly shuts down for any reason, your copy will not be lost.

1) Transfer your outline to the screen to guide your writing. Do this in one of two ways. In the first, place your outline on the screen and write material under each heading as you develop ideas. Many of the headings will serve as topic sentences. Transfer your notes as necessary to specific locations under the outline headings.

Method two requires a word processing system that supports windows; that is, the computer splits the screen so that you can write text while another section of the screen, a window, holds in place a section of your outline or a section of your notes. The information in the window helps you write the text, as shown below.

```
I. Television's influence on children
   A. The problem is television's influence on children
   and, in particular, its effects on the language
   development of young people.
```

Without doubt, television influences the mental processes and speaking habits of young people who may develop their language skills in the family den as much as they do in the classroom.

2) Transfer your notes to the text without retyping them. If you used the word processor to write your notes into a single file, such as NOTES, begin writing your draft at the beginning of this NOTES file (which will push your notes downward as you type). When you need a certain note, scroll downward to find it, mark it as a block, scroll upward to your text, and move it into place. Then blend it into your textual discussion with necessary rewording. An important alternative for a long set of notes, 12 or more, would be to label each note with a brief heading so that when you need one, you can employ the FIND feature, block the note, and move it into your text. Keep a separate, written list of these special headings.

If you developed each note as a separate file using a different code word for each, you can pause during your writing and ask the computer to READ or COPY a file into your text. For example, let's suppose you have labeled and filed your notes by number, name of author, or the key words of your outline, such as TVTIME, TVABUSE, THESIS, TV&LANG (Note: names of files are generally limited to eight characters). You would now retrieve these files and blend them into your rough draft. This system is more rapid than the first because you will not scroll through note after note looking for the right one. However, you must keep a written record of file names and the contents of each file.

3) If appropriate to your topic, you can create graphic designs and transfer them into your text. Some computers allow you to create bar, line, or pie graphs as well as spreadsheets, clip art, and original designs. After its creation, transfer the graphic design to your file in an appropriate place. Insert it onto a page if it fits easily. Place a full–page table or illustration on a separate sheet, but make reference to it, such as "see Table 7." Place graphic designs in an appendix only when you have several complex items that would distract readers from your textual message. Remember, however, not to substitute graphics for good solid writing or use them to decorate pages when your information is shaky.

Revising your first computer draft

The word processor enables you to make major and minor changes in the text and then quickly print various drafts of the paper. Consider the following:

Using global revision of the whole work

Once you keyboard the entire paper, you can redesign and realign sentences, paragraphs, and entire pages. Move and rearrange material with the MOVE or MOVE BLOCK commands. After each move remember to rewrite and blend the words into your text. Then reformat your paragraph. Use the FIND command to locate some words and phrases in order to eliminate constant scrolling up and down the screen. Use the FIND/REPLACE to change wording or spelling throughout the document.

Editing your text

In some situations you may have a software program that judges the style of your draft. Such a program tells you: the total number of words, the number of sentences, the average sentence length in words, the number of paragraphs, and the average length of paragraphs in words. It provides a list of your most active words and counts the number of monosyllabic and polysyllabic words. It may locate passive constructions, jargon words, and usage errors. Its analysis then suggests, for example, "Your short paragraphs suggest a journalistic style that may not be appropriate for scholarly writing." You would then revise and edit the text to improve certain stylistic weaknesses.

Some software programs will flag other specific items for correction, such as parentheses that you have opened but not closed, unpaired quotation marks, and passive verbs. A spelling checker will move through your text to flag misspelled words and words not in the computer's dictionary, such as proper names. Some programs suggest correct spellings. Whether such sophisticated software is available or not, you should work through the text on the screen of your monitor and make all necessary editorial changes.

In particular, use the SEARCH function of your computer system and/or the FIND and REPLACE function, either of which moves the cursor quickly to troublesome words and common grammatical errors. For example, if you make mistakes with *there, their,* and *they're,* SEARCH for these words. By concentrating on one problem and tracing it through the entire paper, you can edit effectively. Following are some problem areas you may want to look for:

1) Words commonly misused Do you sometimes use *alot* rather than *a lot* and *to* rather than *too?* If so, order a SEARCH for *alot* and then for *to* and correct errors accordingly. You know your weaknesses, so search out usage problems that plague you:

accept/except	*lay/lie*
adapt/adopt	*criteria/criterion*
on to/onto	*advice/advise*
data/datum	*passed/past*
all ready/already	*farther/further*
suppose to/supposed to	*among/between*
its/it's	*use to/used to*

Remember, these are words a spelling checker will usually ignore, so the SEARCH is necessary.

2) Contractions Research papers are formal, so avoid contractions. You can easily correct them by a SEARCH for the apostrophe (').

3) Pronouns Troublesome words are *he, she, it, they, their* because referents can be unclear. For example, SEARCH *he* to be sure you have a clear masculine referent, not ambiguity or bias:

```
Stonewall Jackson served General Lee valiantly
in the battles against Union forces. He was a
man of raw courage.
```

The cursor blinking as it pauses at *He* encourages a change to:

```
Stonewall Jackson served General Lee valiantly
in the battles against Union forces. Jackson,
like Lee, was a man of raw courage.
```

A SEARCH for the word *this* might uncover this error:

```
Himmelweit stresses this point: "Book reading
comes into its own, not despite television but
because of it" (qtd. in Postman 33). This is
questioned by some authorities.
```

The first highlighted *this* is correct, but the second needs editing:

```
This view by Himmelweit is questioned by some
authorities.
```

4) Unnecessary negatives SEARCH for *no, not, never* in order to correct unclear, negative wording:

```
A not unacceptable reading of Hawthorne is
Fogle's interpretation of The Scarlet Letter.
```

Editing can change the sentence to a positive assertion:

```
Fogle's reading of The Scarlet Letter asserts
Hawthorne's positive view of Hester's moral
strength (15).
```

5) Punctuation SEARCH for the comma (,) and the semicolon (;) to establish your accuracy. Check your use of quotation marks to open and to close your quotations. If you employ parentheses regularly, SEARCH for the opening parentheses and check visually for a closing one.

6) Abbreviations Use the SEARCH AND REPLACE function to put into final form any abbreviated words or phrases employed in the early draft(s). For example, you might have saved time in drafting the paper by typing SL for *The Scarlet Letter*. Now is the time to SEARCH for each instance of SL and to replace it automatically with the full title.

Proofreading the computer printout

After you have edited the text to your satisfaction, print a copy as formatted by your final specifications, such as double spacing, one-inch margins, page numbers, and so forth. Proofread this version for correctness of format and spelling, punctuation, alphabetizing of the "Works Cited" page, and so forth. If at all possible, print your final version on a laser printer or a typewriter-quality printer. Such printers, with sheet-fed paper or razor-cut continuous forms paper, will produce a manuscript of the best typewriter quality.

Matters of Mechanics

Abbreviations. Employ abbreviations often and consistently in notes and citations, but avoid them in the text. In documentation abbreviate dates (Jan. or Dec.), institutions (acad. and assn.), names of publishers (UP for University Press), and states (OH or CA).

Accents. When you quote, reproduce accents exactly as they appear in the original. Use ink if your typewriter or word processor does not support the marks.

Arabic Numerals. MLA style demands Arabic numerals whenever possible: for volumes, books, parts, and chapters of works; acts, scenes, and lines of plays; cantos, stanzas, and lines of poetry. Write as Arabic numerals any numbers below 10 that cannot be spelled out in one or two words (such as 3 1/2 or 6.234). Numbers below 10 grouped with higher numbers should appear as Arabic numerals (such as "3 out of 42 subjects" or "lines 6 and 13" but "15 tests in three categories"). Large numbers may combine numerals and words (such as 3.5 million). For inclusive numbers that indicate a range, give the second number in full for numbers through 99: 3–5, 15–21, 70–96. MLA style: With three digits or more give only last two in the second number unless more digits are needed for clarity: **98–101, 110–12, 989–1001, 1030–33, 2766–854.** APA style: With three digits or more give all numbers: **110–112, 1030–1033, 2766–2854.** Spell out the initial number that begins a sentence, e.g., "Thirty people participated in the initial test.".

Capitalization. Titles of books, journals, magazines, and newspapers: capitalize the first word and all principal words, but not articles, prepositions, conjunctions, and the *to* in infinitives, when these words occur in the middle of the title (for example, *The Last of the Mohicans*). Titles of articles and parts of books: capitalize as for books. If the first line of a poem serves as the title, reproduce it exactly as it appears in print ("anyone lived in a pretty how town").

Indenting. Indent paragraphs of your text five spaces. Indent long quotations 10 spaces. The opening sentence to a quoted paragraph receives no extra indentation; however, if you quote two or more paragraphs, indent the beginning of each paragraph an extra three spaces. Indent "Works Cited" entries five spaces on the second and succeeding lines. Indent the first line of content footnotes five spaces. Other styles (APA) have different requirements (see Chapter 11).

Italics. If your word processing system and your printer will reproduce italic lettering, use it. Otherwise, show italics in a typed or handwritten manuscript by underlining.

Monetary Units. Spell out percentages and monetary amounts only if you can do so in no more than two words. For example, *$10 or ten dollars.*

Percentages. Use numerals with appropriate symbols (3%, $5.60); otherwise use numerals only when they cannot be spelled out in one or two words. For example, *one hundred percent but 150 percent.* In business, scientific, and technical writing that requires frequent use of percentages, write all percentages as numerals with appropriate symbols.

Short Titles in the Text. Use abbreviated titles of books and articles mentioned often in the text after a first, full reference. For example, *Backgrounds to English as Language* should be shortened, after initial usage, to *Backgrounds* both in the text, notes, and in-text citations but not in the bibliography entry.

Underlining for emphasis. On occasion, you may use underlining to emphasize certain words or phrases in a typed paper, but positioning the key word accomplishes the same purpose:
Expressed Emphasis: Perhaps an answer lies in *preventing* abuse, not in makeshift remedies after the fact.
Better: Prevention of abuse is a better answer than makeshift remedies after the fact.

INDEX